MODIFYING YOUR THINKING CLASSROOM FOR DIFFERENT SETTINGS

MODIFYING YOUR THINKING CLASSROOM FOR DIFFERENT SETTINGS

A Supplement to

Building Thinking Classrooms in Mathematics

Peter Liljedahl

Illustrations by Laura Wheeler

CORWIN Mathematics

For information:

Corwin
A SAGE Company
2455 Teller Road
Thousand Oaks, California 91320
(800) 233-9936
www.corwin.com

SAGE Publications Ltd.
1 Oliver's Yard
55 City Road
London EC1Y 1SP
United Kingdom

SAGE Publications India Pvt. Ltd.
B 1/I 1 Mohan Cooperative
    Industrial Area
Mathura Road, New Delhi 110 044
India

SAGE Publications Asia-Pacific Pte. Ltd.
18 Cross Street #10-10/11/12
China Square Central
Singapore 048423

President: Mike Soules
*Associate Vice President and Editorial
    Director:* Monica Eckman
Publisher: Erin Null
Content Development Editor:
    Jessica Vidal
Senior Editorial Assistant:
    Caroline Timmings
Production Editor: Melanie Birdsall
Typesetter: Integra
Proofreader: Wendy Jo Dymond
Cover Designer: Candice Harman
Marketing Manager: Margaret O'Connor

ISBN 978-1-0718-5784-7

24 25 10 9 8 7 6

CONTENTS

ABOUT THE AUTHOR

Dr. Peter Liljedahl is a professor of mathematics education at Simon Fraser University in Vancouver, Canada. He is the current president of the Canadian Mathematics Education Study Group (CMESG), past-president of the International Group for the Psychology of Mathematics Education (IGPME), editor of the *International Journal of Science and Mathematics Education* (IJSME), on the editorial board of five major international journals, and a member of the National Council of Teachers of Mathematics (NCTM) Research Committee. Peter has authored or co-authored numerous books, book chapters, and journal articles on topics central to the teaching and learning of mathematics. He is a former high school mathematics teacher who has kept his research close to the classroom and consults regularly with teachers, schools, school districts, ministries of education, and universities on issues of teaching and learning, assessment, and numeracy. Peter is a sought-after presenter who has given talks all over the world on the topic of building thinking classrooms, for which he has won the Cmolik Prize for the Enhancement of Public Education and the Fields Institute's Margaret Sinclair Memorial Award for Innovation and Excellence in Mathematics Education.

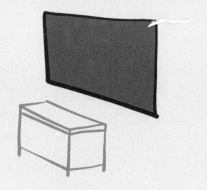

INTRODUCTION

Building Thinking Classrooms is a framework for teaching that emerged out of 15 years of work with teachers in classrooms. The result of this work is published in the anchor book, *Building Thinking Classrooms in Mathematics, Grades K–12: 14 Teaching Practices for Enhancing Learning.* That book briefly shares the inception of the idea and then talks about the 14 practices that the research shows have the most potential to increase student thinking in the classroom.

The supplement that you are now reading looks at how to adapt these practices to build thinking classrooms in settings other than the typical face-to-face setting described in the anchor book. Some of these settings have existed for a long time. Other settings emerged during the COVID-19 pandemic as ways to keep learning moving forward while adhering to regional and federal safety guidelines. In this supplement, I look at 12 such settings, divided into five categories.

Category 1: Face-to-Face Learning Environments

1. Building a Thinking Classroom With Social Distancing

2. Building a Thinking Classroom With Fixed Seating

3. Building a Thinking Classroom With Small Class Sizes

Category 2: Virtual Learning Environments

4. Building a Thinking Classroom for a Synchronous Virtual Setting

5. Building a Thinking Classroom in an Asynchronous Virtual Setting

Category 3: Hybrid Learning Environments

6. Building a Thinking Classroom for an Asynchronous Hybrid Setting

7. Building a Thinking Classroom for a Synchronous Hybrid Setting

Category 4: Other Learning Environments

8. Building a Thinking Classroom for Independent Learning

9. Building a Thinking Classroom for Homeschooling

Category 5: Supporting Learners

10. Supporting Students With Unfinished Learning of Previous Concepts in a Thinking Classroom

11. Supporting Students With Unfinished Learning of Current Concepts in a Thinking Classroom

12. Supporting Students Through One-on-One Teaching Using Thinking Classroom Practices

Each of these chapters begins with a detailed description of the setting that it is written about. I hope that whatever setting you are teaching in matches one of these. But the spectrum of what teaching and learning can look like is wide. So, there is a chance that your work as a teacher takes place in a setting other than what is captured in this supplement—for example, small classes with fixed seating. If this is the case, I am hopeful that you will be able to combine ideas from different chapters to be able to still build a thinking classroom within your unique situation.

Some of these settings require the adaptations of just a few of the 14 thinking classroom practices. Others will require adaptations of more than a few. And almost all of them require an adaptation in the order in which the practices are implemented.

14 TEACHING PRACTICES FOR ENHANCING LEARNING

1. Give thinking tasks.
2. Frequently form visibly random groups.
3. Use vertical non-permanent surfaces.
4. Defront the classroom.
5. Answer only keep-thinking questions.
6. Give thinking task early, standing, and verbally.
7. Give check-your-understanding questions.
8. Mobilize knowledge.
9. Asynchronously use hints and extensions to maintain flow.
10. Consolidate from the bottom.
11. Have students write meaningful notes.
12. Evaluate what you value.
13. Help students see where they are and where they are going.
14. Grade based on data (not points).

HOW TO READ THIS SUPPLEMENT

The first working assumption is that you are familiar with the anchor book, so this supplement will make the most sense if you have read that. The second assumption is that you will not read this cover to cover but will consult the chapters most relevant to your situation at any given time.

The first nine chapters present the adaptations that are necessary to build a thinking classroom within that particular setting. For example, Chapter 1 looks at building a thinking classroom in a setting where students are face to face, but there is a restriction that requires them to maintain a social distance. All 14 of the thinking practices in the anchor book are still relevant to this setting, but four of them will need to be adapted to be effective within this context. What is discussed in Chapter 1, then, are the four practices that need adaptation and what adaptations are necessary. What is not discussed are the 10 practices that can still be enacted as in the anchor book.

Chapters 10 through 12 are different in that they are about how to use some of the thinking classroom practices within various situations where you are offering students support. These chapters only discuss the practices that are relevant.

Once you identify the setting(s) most relevant to your particular context, you can simply read the relevant chapter(s). While it may appear that there is some redundancy between some chapters, be aware that many adaptations are only partially similar and have some aspects that are unique. For example, there is a similarity between how consolidation is modified in Chapters 6 and 7. But there are also a lot of differences between these two adaptations. Do not assume that because you are familiar with the adaptations for one setting that you know the adaptations for the other.

The other modification you'll see is to the order that practices should be implemented for each of these 12 settings. As such, each chapter ends with a modified pseudo-sequenced order of implementation. In some cases, this modification results in more toolkits. In others, it results in fewer.

The ideas that are presented in each of these 12 chapters come from a number of different sources. In some cases, they are extrapolations of the over 15 years of face-to-face research that produced the results presented in the anchor book. In other cases, they are the results of having field-tested these modifications in these types of settings described in this supplement. And in other cases, they are a combination of both—extrapolations and field testing. But in no case is the ideas grounded in the kinds of long-term and robust empirical research that the anchor book is based on. Having said that, we are in the same state we were while doing the research into how to build thinking classrooms in face-to-face settings. We have tried some things, we have learned some things, and we have more things to try. So, rather than reading this supplement as the result of a long journey, read it as a journey still in progress. And join in on the journey. Join in on the research. Try it, learn from it, adapt, and try again. In short, use the ideas that are here to begin your own research into how to build a thinking classroom within your own unique classroom setting.

GLOSSARY OF TERMS

There are a number of terms used throughout this supplement that would be useful for you to understand upfront.

Anchor book: The anchor book is the original book written about how to build thinking classrooms—*Building Thinking Classrooms in Mathematics, Grades K–12: 14 Teaching Practices for Enhancing Learning.* It is the book to which this is a supplement.

Asynchronous: This means *not* at the same time. For example, if you are teaching in an asynchronous online setting, this means that your students are accessing you and the course resources at different times from each other.

Hybrid: This is where some of your students are in person in the classroom and some of your students are elsewhere (typically at home). In some hybrid settings, the students that are at home are connecting virtually and synchronously to what is happening in the face-to-face lesson. Other times, they are not connecting at all or are connecting asynchronously to what is happening in the face-to-face lesson.

Jamboard: A Jamboard is a Google-based digital whiteboard that allows students to draw with a stylus or a mouse, add text boxes or sticky notes, add images, and erase. It also allows for students to use text boxes, sticky notes, and images as manipulatives.

Knowledgefeed: A knowledgefeed is, in essence, a chat window with the capability to post text, images, and screen captures in a linear and non-chronological order. A knowledgefeed is populated with things that students would see on vertical non-permanent surfaces (VNPSs) in a face-to-face setting.

Normal: Despite the fact that there is no such thing as a normal thinking classroom, this description is sometimes used in this supplement to distinguish between the settings presented in this supplement and the face-to-face synchronous setting described in the anchor book.

Online: This is a reference to how students are connecting to you, the lesson, or the course resources through the internet.

Supplement: What you are reading now is the supplement. Think of it as an appendix to the anchor book.

Synchronous: This means at the same time. For example, if you are teaching in a synchronous online setting, this means that all of your students are connecting at the same time.

Unfinished learning: This is a phenomenon wherein a student has not yet learned mathematics that they have been exposed to. All students have learning that is unfinished. In some cases, they have minimal and recent unfinished learning. In other cases, the unfinished learning is more substantial and could relate to concepts they were exposed to a long time ago.

Virtual: *See* Online.

KNOWLEDGEFEED

One of the big advantages of having students work on vertical non-permanent surfaces (VPNSs) in a "normal" or typical face-to-face classroom is that it so well facilitates the movement of knowledge between groups. When groups get stuck, they can passively look to the work of others to get a hint—whether that hint is a type of notation, a way to organize data, a partial solution, or a path to a solution. Alternatively, if a group has completed a problem or task, they can passively look around the room to get an extension to the task from another group. If this passive interaction with the work of other groups is inadequate, a group may choose to more actively engage with that group by asking for help or interrogating them about things they have seen in their work but do not fully understand. Whether passive or active, this gathering of hints and extensions creates a type of knowledge mobility that is instrumental in helping keep groups in flow as they work through a series of curricular or non-curricular tasks.

In many of the settings discussed in this supplement, we can still do random groups, and we can use digital whiteboards in place of VNPSs. The problem is that these digital whiteboards do not allow for the same level of passive interaction that a glance over your shoulder in a face-to-face classroom affords. To compensate for this, you can make a *knowledgefeed*. A knowledgefeed is just a collaborative GoogleDoc that you create and that students keep open on their desktop while working in certain settings and is populated with the kinds of things that students would see on VNPSs in a face-to-face classroom. This includes everything from the task at hand to hints, extensions, and (pictures of) student work. When you first start to use a knowledgefeed in your setting, it is something that you, as the teacher, posts to. However, in many settings, it becomes advantageous to work toward having students also post to it. They can post their own images of work, hints, questions, and answers to questions.

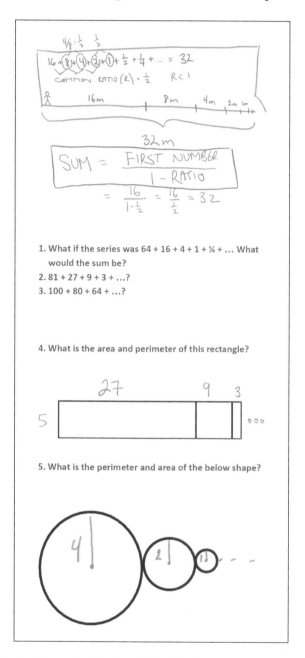

Figure i.1   An Example of a Knowledgefeed

In Chapters 2, 4, 5, 6, and 7 of this supplement, I discuss very specific ways to set up and organize a knowledgefeed as well as how to move students toward using it as a source for knowledge mobility.

CATEGORY 1

FACE-TO-FACE LEARNING ENVIRONMENTS

1

BUILDING A THINKING CLASSROOM WITH SOCIAL DISTANCING

. . . .

Something that may stay with us for a long time after the COVID-19 pandemic is a pervasive and ongoing need to keep our students three to six feet apart from each other. What would a thinking classroom look like in such an environment? Interestingly, all the thinking classroom practices are still relevant, important, and achievable. While most practices can stay the same in a socially distanced classroom, what changes are where students stand and how they move. There are four practices specifically that need some modification.

WHERE STUDENTS WORK IN A THINKING CLASSROOM

Practice 3

Despite the need for social distancing, we still want students to work at vertical non-permanent surfaces (VNPSs). However, we need them to do so while maintaining distance from each other. The easiest way to achieve this is to use masking tape to mark out an equilateral triangle on the floor at each workstation. The length of each side of the triangle should be the distance apart that students need to remain, and only one vertex of the triangle should be at the VNPS. While working on the VNPS, students are to stand at these tape marks (see Figure 1.1).

Figure 1.1 Masking Tape Triangle at VNPS

This triangle setup may require you to reconfigure your VNPSs around the room. If you previously had five or six groups along one wall of your classroom, using the triangle configuration may mean you can now only fit three. Luckily, your classroom has four walls. Make use of these to spread your workstations around the room. This means that, even if you have wall-to-wall whiteboards on two or three of your walls, you will have to improvise to get VNPSs onto your previously unused vertical spaces. Keep in mind that there are many products available to you for this improvisation (blackboards, windows, vinyl picnic table covers, cellophane, Wipeboards by Wipebooks, Better than Paper by Teacher Created Resources, and Dry Erase Surface by Post-It).

The triangle setup not only maintains distance between students but also ensures that only one student is writing on the VNPS at a time. Whether each student has their own marker or they share a marker, having only one student writing at a time was clearly shown to enhance the collaboration that takes place within groups. But who is writing also needs to change over time. Just like in a normal thinking classroom, this is facilitated in one of two ways:

1. From time to time, you may ask that students change who is writing. You can do this synchronously (asking every group to make a change at the same time) or asynchronously (asking a particular group to change who is writing based on what you see is going on within the group).

2. Ask groups to manage this on their own, deciding for themselves who is writing in the same way they would if they were all at the VNPSs in a non–socially distanced thinking classroom.

Regardless of how it is done, however, you can change who is writing by simply rotating the triangle, either clockwise or counterclockwise, to bring a new writer to the VNPS. If you are controlling this rotation synchronously, try to specify which direction this rotation should always follow to make sure everyone gets a chance to write. In other cases, which direction the rotation happens has more to do with which student you, or the group, wants at the board. For both methods, you can still require that whoever is writing is not allowed to write their own ideas and can only act as a scribe for the ideas of their group mates.

HOW WE ARRANGE THE FURNITURE IN A THINKING CLASSROOM

Practice 4

Keeping students at a distance while working at their VNPS is one thing. You also need to keep them apart when they are at their desks. When configuring the desks to accommodate this, keep in mind that you still want to defront your classroom by having students face every which way. This will send the message to the students that your classroom is a safe space to think.

Defronting your classroom while creating a distance between desks, coupled with the creation of the equilateral triangles at each vertical workstation, may require more floor space than your classroom currently has available, and "there is no way to just fit it all in." The easy solution to this lies in the realization that students are not both sitting at their desks and working at their VNPSs at the same time. It is okay if their desks overlap the VNPS triangles while they are seated. When it is time to work at their vertical workstations, they just need to move their desks away from the walls. And vice versa—when it is time to sit again, they move their desks back. Some teachers have facilitated this fluid use of space by marking the position of these mobile desks on the floor using a different color masking tape. Yes, your classroom floor is going to start to look like a gymnasium floor with some lines marking out the volleyball court and others marking out the basketball court. But the students learn quickly which lines are relevant for standing and which are relevant for sitting.

WHEN, WHERE, AND HOW TASKS ARE GIVEN IN A THINKING CLASSROOM

Practice 6

As in a normal thinking classroom setting, you give tasks early, verbally, and with the students standing. But with the need for social distancing, students are not standing in that same huddle around you. Although not ideal, this is best done with the students already at their vertical workstations in their triangular positions. With the students spread around the perimeter of the room, and to create as much proximal access as possible, you should then be in the middle of the room talking and demonstrating the task. This means, unlike in a normal setting, you need to form random groups before giving the task. It also means that, if you need to write down parts of the task as part of the demonstration, there either needs to be a whiteboard on a rotating easel in the middle of the room or a whiteboard around the perimeter that you can use. Alternatively, you can be writing on a tablet that projects to a screen. As much as possible, however, you need to be physically in the middle of the room talking to the students around the perimeter. Despite the need for social distancing, your proximity to students when giving the task is still important. The further you are from the students, the more likely they are to feel anonymous and disengage.

HOW WE CONSOLIDATE A LESSON IN A THINKING CLASSROOM

Practice 10

The need to keep students on their feet and in proximity to you is also an important part of how you consolidate the lesson. Regardless of which of the three methods for consolidation you use—(1) discussion with nothing written down, (2) discussion with you recording what is discussed, or (3) discussion of student work—the need to socially distance creates challenges for this practice. You can easily achieve the first of these by having the students stay in the triangles at their workstations while you move about in the middle of the room. The second can be done in the same way you gave the task, with the students at their vertical workstations and you in the middle of the room writing on an easel or a tablet.

The third, and most important, form of consolidation—using students' work—is trickier. An easy, and tempting, fix for this is to take pictures of student VNPSs while they are working and to use these to lead a consolidation while they are in their seats. The problem is that the minute they are sitting, the disengagement happens. The original research into thinking classrooms clearly showed this. Alternatively, you can keep students at their vertical workstations and have them pivot their attention as you move from workstation to workstation, unpacking the salient parts of the activity through the use of student work. The problem here is that this maintains the attachment between the work and the students who produced it in a way that our original research showed was problematic. The solution then is to have all the groups rotate two to three workstations clockwise (or counterclockwise) under the pretense that they are to try to interpret what a different group was thinking. After you have given them a few minutes to do this, you can begin your consolidation. This rotation has effectively severed their attachment to, and ownership of, their own work. This both increases the anonymity of the work and allows you to take ownership of the gallery for your own purposes. And the purpose, in this case, is to use student work to consolidate from the bottom. This method of severing connection through rotation still keeps the students at a distance from each other and allows you to effectively integrate and layer all three types of consolidation.

TOOLKITS

In a socially distanced thinking classroom, the toolkits are the same as they are in a normal thinking classroom (see Figure 1.2).

- Give thinking tasks.
- Frequently form visibly random groups.
- Use vertical non-permanent surfaces.

- Defront the classroom.
- Answer only keep-thinking questions.
- Give thinking task early, standing, and verbally.
- Give check-your-understanding questions.
- Mobilize knowledge.

- Asynchronously use hints and extensions to maintain flow.
- Consolidate from the bottom.
- Have students write meaningful notes.

- Evaluate what you value.
- Help students see where they are and where they are going.
- Grade based on data (not points).

Figure 1.2 Toolkits for Building a Thinking Classroom With Social Distancing

2

BUILDING A THINKING CLASSROOM WITH FIXED SEATING

. . . .

One of the ways social distancing has been enacted has been to require students to stay in their seats. In some cases, this means students have to be in the same seat for an extended period and/or that they always have to be front-facing. In other cases, students can sit in different seats from one day to the next and/or the desks can be clustered and face different directions. Regardless of how frequently seats can be changed or how desks can be clustered, these restrictions necessitate modifications to 10 of the thinking classroom practices.

This context also requires the use of a knowledgefeed as described in the introduction. There should be a single and unique knowledgefeed for each lesson that will be used primarily as a place to post tasks, extensions, and screen captures of interesting work. It will also be a place through which you will lead the consolidation and, as such, should be projected on a screen in the classroom.

Practice 2

HOW GROUPS ARE FORMED IN A THINKING CLASSROOM

Regardless of when and how seating is arranged, in a setting where students must stay seated, groups will comprise the students who are in proximity to each other. For example, the three desks in the front corner of the room are a group (see Figure 2.1).

Figure 2.1 Groups in a Row Arrangement of Desks

If students are able to vary their seats from day to day, then who works with what group is determined by where they sit. This can still be randomized either using cards as they come in the door or with the use of a digital random group generator. If students have to remain in their seats for extended or indefinite periods (meaning more than one class period), then who works in a group can be determined by which desks will form a group. And this can change from day to day. The easiest way to achieve this is to have several desk grouping charts (see Figure 2.2) that you cycle through from one day to the next.

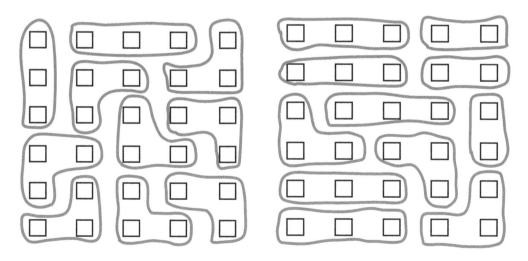

Figure 2.2 Multiple Grouping Arrangements

Three students to a group (as in Figures 2.1 and 2.2) is still ideal. But this is largely dependent on how far apart the desks are. If the desks are far apart by necessity, you may need to go to pairs to keep the proximity between students reasonable. Or you may need to use a combination of groups of two and three. Of course, this is all made more complex by the eventuality of student absences, so you always need to be willing to adapt your grouping plans and be flexible around the need for close proximity.

WHERE STUDENTS WORK IN A THINKING CLASSROOM

Practice 3

Once seated and in their groups, students will need a work surface to show their shared thinking. This can be achieved in one of three ways:

1. **Shared Whiteboards.** This is just a whiteboard that one of the group members uses to scribe what the group is talking about. Ideally, the student doing the writing can hold the board vertically on their desk so their group mates can see it. More likely, what will happen is that the board will repeatedly move from being laid flat when being written on to vertical for the other group members to see what has been written. In some cases, it may be possible to have students pass the whiteboard between each other, either at the groups' discretion or at your insistence.

2. **Individual Whiteboards.** In this case, students can each have their own whiteboard on which they write ideas that they can share with their group. Interestingly, this option often morphs, quite naturally, into the first option, where one students' whiteboard becomes the shared representational space where all the students in the group focus their attention.

3. **Digital Whiteboards.** Another option is to use a cloud-based digital whiteboard. There are several available for free and they are not hard to find, but the one that I have found works best is Jamboard. Jamboard is and always will be free—which is not always true of other products. It allows students to draw with a stylus or a mouse, add text boxes or sticky

notes, add images, and erase. It even allows for students to use text boxes, sticky notes, and images as manipulatives. Finally, it allows all members of a group to work inside the same representational space at the same time, which nicely emulates the work at a vertical non-permanent surface (VNPS). The other nice feature is that if a group runs out of space, they can just add (or move to) another frame. Each Jamboard link can have up to 20 frames (see Figure 2.3).

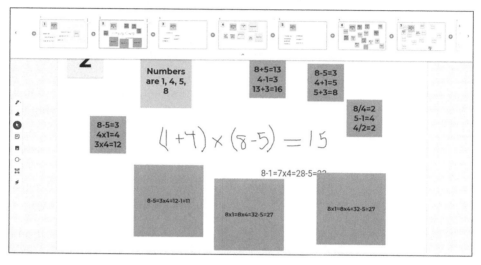

Figure 2.3 A Jamboard With Multiple Frames

Source: Created using Google Jamboard.

Jamboard is a Google product and, like other Google products, is purported to be able to handle 100 viewers at a time. This is true. However, if all those viewers also have editor privileges, then Jamboard gets buggy. We have found that if you keep the number of editors to 15 or below, then the platform is very stable. So, you will need to create multiple Jamboard links and have a maximum of five groups working on each link.

When students work on a VNPS in person, there is the restriction that there is only one whiteboard marker per group. Even in a socially distanced classroom where every student may have their own marker, there is only one student at the board at a time. These restrictions have been shown to enhance collaboration. On Jamboard, every student has the ability to write at the same time. This is also true when they work on individual whiteboards. So, take extra care to establish appropriate collaborative behaviors in these settings (see Practice 12).

HOW WE ANSWER QUESTIONS IN A THINKING CLASSROOM

Practice 5

In many ways, answering questions in a thinking classroom with fixed seating restrictions is the same as in a regular thinking classroom—you do not answer proximity and stop-thinking questions. But you have to be more vigilant about what students are asking, how to respond to the question, and what to do afterward. In a regular thinking classroom, if you get it wrong—for example, you mistake a keep-thinking question for a proximity question and smile and walk away—the student or group who asked the question can consult the other groups around them. If you have done a good job building the autonomy to access these resources, the number of questions (of any type) that you get decreases, and the need to respond to them correctly is less important. That is not true in a thinking classroom with fixed seating. The inability for students to access other groups' work, and to actively engage with other groups around their work, is severely depleted. Students have access to fewer resources in these types of settings.

So, we have to get it more right. If you cannot decide if a question is a proximity question or a keep-thinking question, err on the side of keep-thinking and answer it. If you choose not to answer the question, circle back and try to see if the group is progressing despite you not answering their question. This is easier said than done. But there is a silver lining among all these restrictions and impediments—the knowledgefeed and the way it can be used to mobilize knowledge in these restricted thinking classrooms (see Practice 8). So, you may wish to direct them to scroll through the knowledgefeed looking for an answer to their question. And you may even choose to add something to the knowledgefeed for them to find. If you get asked the same question multiple times or anticipate needing to answer a question multiple times, add an answer, in the form of a hint, to the knowledgefeed.

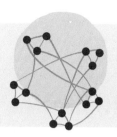

HOW WE FOSTER STUDENT AUTONOMY IN A THINKING CLASSROOM

Practice 8

In a thinking classroom, you want to foster knowledge mobility—students' autonomy to get knowledge from other groups. In a normal thinking classroom, students achieve this by passively glancing at other groups' vertical work and actively engaging other groups in discussion about their work. In a thinking classroom with fixed seating, passive engagement is still possible through the use of the knowledgefeed. Irrespective of what kind of collaborative workspace the groups are using—group whiteboards, individual whiteboards, or digital whiteboards—the knowledgefeed creates a space that students can quickly glance at to gain a hint if they are stuck or an extension if they are ready to move on. Jamboards, with five groups to a single Jamboard, also offer the possibility for groups to passively glance at each other's work. To move this glancing beyond the specific Jamboard a group is working in, all the Jamboard links in use should be published on the knowledgefeed.

As we learned in the original research into building thinking classrooms, however, making the knowledge available is not enough—you need to help students access this knowledge. And as discussed in the anchor book, talking to students about this is not enough. You need to force them to access it by being deliberately less helpful. So, rather than answering their questions, direct them to a place in the knowledgefeed or on the Jamboards to find what they are looking for. This, coupled with specific attention to student behavior (see Practice 12), will increase knowledge mobility even in this restricted thinking classroom environment.

WHAT WE CHOOSE TO EVALUATE IN A THINKING CLASSROOM

Practice 12

The fixed seating restriction requires students to behave in specific ways in order for these thinking classroom adaptations to be effective. One of the best ways to shape these behaviors is to evaluate what we value. And what we value in a thinking classroom with fixed seating is that students are as attentive when the task is given out and when consolidation is going on as they would be if they were on their feet. This means students have to be more responsible for their actions. To help with this, co-construct rubrics around what it means to be an engaged learner, or an attentive listener, or ready to learn. You can also build rubrics around what it means to gather ideas or what to do when stuck or finished or how to be an effective group. This last rubric could also include language around how to take turns writing regardless of what kind of work surface students are using—group whiteboards, individual whiteboards, or digital whiteboards. The focus on who is writing can also be in rubrics around collaboration, or whiteboard etiquette, and so on. In short, just like in a normal thinking classroom, identify behaviors you would like to see changed and co-construct rubrics around these.

HOW WE ARRANGE THE FURNITURE (KNOWLEDGEFEED) IN A THINKING CLASSROOM

Practice 4

If the requirement for fixed seating plans does not also require that the desks be in rows, then defronting the classroom as stated in the anchor book is easy. In fact, it is easier because there is not the need to defront the classroom while also trying to ensure that there is enough room around the perimeter to access the VNPSs.

If the desks need to be in rows, however, there is not much you can do to defront the classroom. But defronting the classroom is only a means to an end. And the end is to introduce enough chaos into the classroom that students perceive it as a safe place to think—to get messy and make mistakes. Defronting the classroom is only one way to achieve this. There are other ways to introduce small amounts of chaos. In a classroom that uses a knowledgefeed, the easiest way to do this is to allow the knowledgefeed to be messy. It is not important that all the information that gets posted on the knowledgefeed be thematically or chronologically organized. The knowledgefeed, like student work, is an artifact of thinking. Thinking is messy and full of errors. Let the knowledgefeed display this.

WHEN, WHERE, AND HOW TASKS ARE GIVEN IN A THINKING CLASSROOM

Practice 6

In thinking classrooms with restricted seating, you still give tasks verbally during the first five minutes of class. However, you cannot give them while students are clustered around you. When students have to remain at their desks, you need to pay extra attention to establishing norms around listening to the instructions (see Practice 12). Once you have given the task, and the groups have started working, place the task on the knowledgefeed in a text light form. That is, whereas the verbal instructions will contain elements of storytelling, narrative, and/or modeling, what you recorded is a simple set of instructions as to what the students are to do. For example, consider the tax collector from Chapter 6 of the anchor book. In this fixed seating context, you would give this task to the students verbally. What you would write on the knowledgefeed, however, is "Using 12 envelopes, try to get more than $22." This sets up the flow sequence discussed in Practice 9 in this chapter.

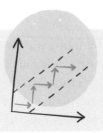

HOW WE USE HINTS AND EXTENSIONS IN A THINKING CLASSROOM

Practice 9

Even with students in fixed seats, you need to maintain flow, but it is much harder to get the timing right. In a normal thinking classroom, all the work that the groups are producing is visible at a glance. This allows a teacher to monitor progress and to interject hints and extensions when needed. Having students in their seats impedes our ability to quickly ascertain where groups are in their progress. So, the groups themselves have to use their ability to mobilize knowledge and maintain flow as they balance their ability and challenge. They need to seek out hints in the knowledgefeed or other Jamboards if they are stuck, or they need to find the next question on the knowledgefeed if they are ready to move on. Your job is still to create the flow sequence of tasks and to add these to the knowledgefeed, one at a time, in pace with the fastest moving groups. To be clear, this does not mean that you should simply post a list of questions on the knowledgefeed. The research clearly shows that this creates a reach-for-the-finish-line behavior that fractures collaboration. To maintain a focus on thinking while groups work on the task at hand, you need to distribute the flow sequence throughout the knowledgefeed among the various hints and images of groups' work.

HOW WE CONSOLIDATE A LESSON IN A THINKING CLASSROOM

Practice 10

In a normal thinking classroom, while students are working through the tasks you are giving out one at a time, you move around the room seeding ideas and locking in work in anticipation of the consolidation that will follow. In the context of fixed seating, this still needs to happen. The difference is that locking-in work is already occurring in the form of photos and screen captures that are being posted to the knowledgefeed—whether by the teacher or by students. As such, the gallery walk will be a guided tour through the knowledgefeed. Like a normal thinking classroom, however, this does not mean that we should showcase all the work. Nor does it mean that we just move through the work linearly. Careful selection and sequencing are still needed to build a narrative that can move students through the various levels of complexity and nuances encountered in the lesson.

Knowing that the knowledgefeed will become the source for the consolidation will invariably begin to shape what it is you, as the teacher, choose to capture and display in the knowledgefeed. It may even begin to shape what students choose to add to the knowledgefeed. But do not allow this reality to overly control the way in which the knowledge emerges. There is still a need for the knowledgefeed to maintain a certain amount of chaos in order to send the message to the students that messiness and errors are part of thinking (see Practice 4).

Practice 11

HOW STUDENTS TAKE NOTES IN A THINKING CLASSROOM

Irrespective of how the consolidation is conducted, students will still need to make meaningful notes for themselves. In the case of fixed seating, the images from the consolidation that are archived on the knowledgefeed will help students produce these notes.

TOOLKITS

In a fixed seating thinking classroom, all 14 practices are still relevant. Some can be executed as usual; others need adaptations. Also in need of adaptation are the orders with which these practices are implements and the toolkits into which they cluster (see Figure 2.4).

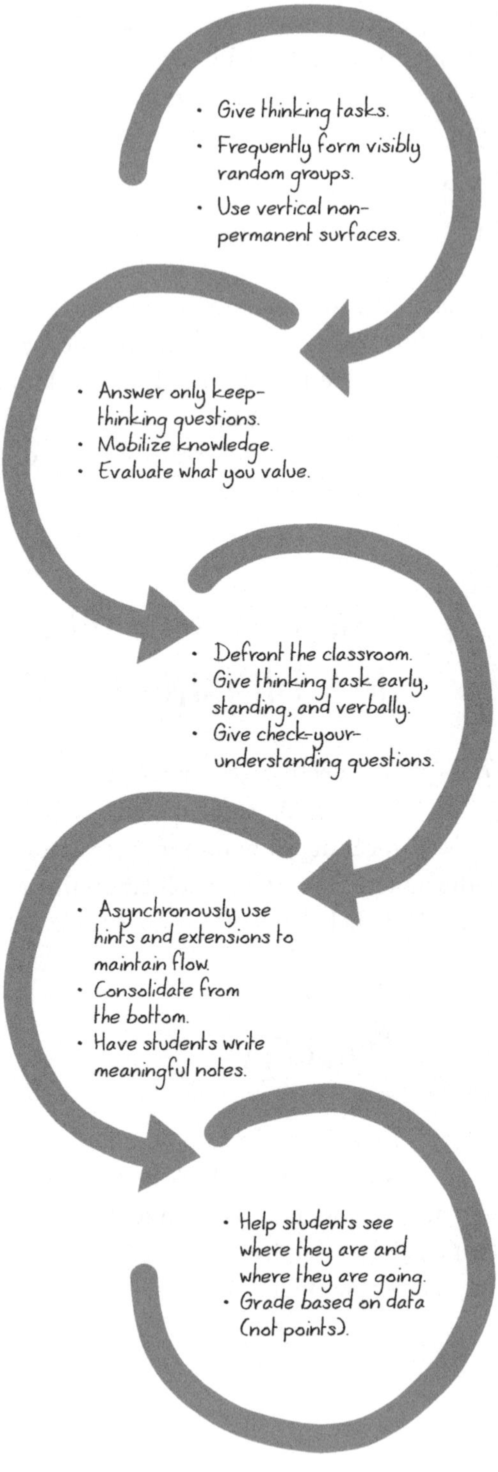

- Give thinking tasks.
- Frequently form visibly random groups.
- Use vertical non-permanent surfaces.

- Answer only keep-thinking questions.
- Mobilize knowledge.
- Evaluate what you value.

- Defront the classroom.
- Give thinking task early, standing, and verbally.
- Give check-your-understanding questions.

- Asynchronously use hints and extensions to maintain flow.
- Consolidate from the bottom.
- Have students write meaningful notes.

- Help students see where they are and where they are going.
- Grade based on data (not points).

Figure 2.4 Toolkits for Building a Thinking Classroom With Fixed Seating

3

BUILDING A THINKING CLASSROOM WITH SMALL CLASS SIZES

· ·

Small classes have existed for a long time. We often see this in the context of very specific elective courses that attract a small number of students, private school settings where the ratio of students to teacher is kept low, or rural settings where the overall school population is small. We may also see more of this as we come out of the COVID-19 pandemic as an effort to maintain social distancing in the classroom.

What constitutes a class size small enough to make a difference in a thinking classroom? In our original research, we found the threshold to be around 12 students. Below this and we noticed that, despite the use of frequent random groupings, the students began to feel like they were working with the same peers over and over again. We also noticed that when the number of students in a class dropped below 12, there was a noticeable difference in the amount of diversity available in the room as a whole. Regardless of whether you have a small or large class, groups of three still provide adequate diversity within each group—something I call intra-group diversity. The problem is that if there are only two to four groups, there is not enough diversity in the ideas between groups in the classroom—or inter-group diversity. This is not a problem with larger classes where we tend to see multiple approaches to the same task, but it can be challenging in a small class. To compensate for this, we need to make adjustments to three of the thinking classroom practices.

HOW GROUPS ARE FORMED IN A THINKING CLASSROOM

Practice 2

To increase the amount of inter-group diversity, you can decrease the size of the groups to two, though recognize that this does decrease the intra-group diversity. To make up for this, these groups of two should work in close proximity to other groups (i.e., having one pair work next to another pair), increasing the likelihood that ideas will spread from one group to another. Ironically, while we know from the original thinking classroom research, that groups of four were not effective, we learned that if we put two groups of two next to each other, then they often spontaneously merged into a group of four that functioned much better than had we put those same students into a group of four to begin with. This spontaneous merging tended to happen when the two groups had different ideas, strategies, or solutions to the task at hand. The diversity in thinking drove the merger. In merging, the pairs were able to preserve both the inter-group and intra-group diversity. Also ironically, we have seen that although students spontaneously merged into a group of four, the students in these small classes did not feel like they were "always working with the same people." I think this has to do with the variety that the initial groups of two created.

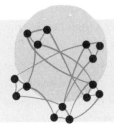

HOW WE FOSTER STUDENT AUTONOMY IN A THINKING CLASSROOM

Practice 8

Whether these small classes of students stay in their groups of two or merge into groups of four, there still is not as much inter-group diversity as we see in larger classes. This means there are fewer ideas for students to access around the room. To compensate for this, you can create vertical non-permanent surface (VNPS) workspace for yourself and use this workspace to display ideas that are not appearing around the room. For example, if no group is making a graph, you make a graph; if no group is solving the task visually, you display it visually; if no group is working backward, you work backward; and so on. The goal is not to work the solution to completion but rather to display ways of thinking, representing, and notating that would appear in larger classes but is not appearing here.

Like in all thinking classrooms, however, merely making knowledge available to students doesn't mean that it moves around. As such, you have to be deliberately less helpful (as discussed in the anchor book) and focus on mobilizing knowledge—which now includes your VNPS—around the room. So, when a group is asking for help, rather than helping them, direct them to VNPS or a group that has the knowledge they are looking for. Likewise, if a group is looking for an extension, rather than giving them the next task, direct them to a VNPS or groups that have the next task.

HOW WE CONSOLIDATE A LESSON IN A THINKING CLASSROOM

Practice 10

Like in any face-to-face thinking classroom, consolidation is done from the bottom. And in this setting, you enact this as described in the anchor book—with careful attention to the selection and sequencing of work to build a cohesive narrative that showcases the evolving complexity of the task(s) at hand. In small classes, the only difference is to also include the work from your own VNPS in this selection and sequencing process. If there are aspects of the consolidation that you wish to discuss that are still absent from the collective work around the room, you can invoke the second type of consolidation activity wherein you lead a detailed discussion about a task and record on a VNPS what the students are telling you.

TOOLKITS

In these small classes, all 14 practices are still relevant. Some can be executed as usual, others need adaptations. But the practices are still enacted in the same order and toolkits as in the anchor book (see Figure 3.1).

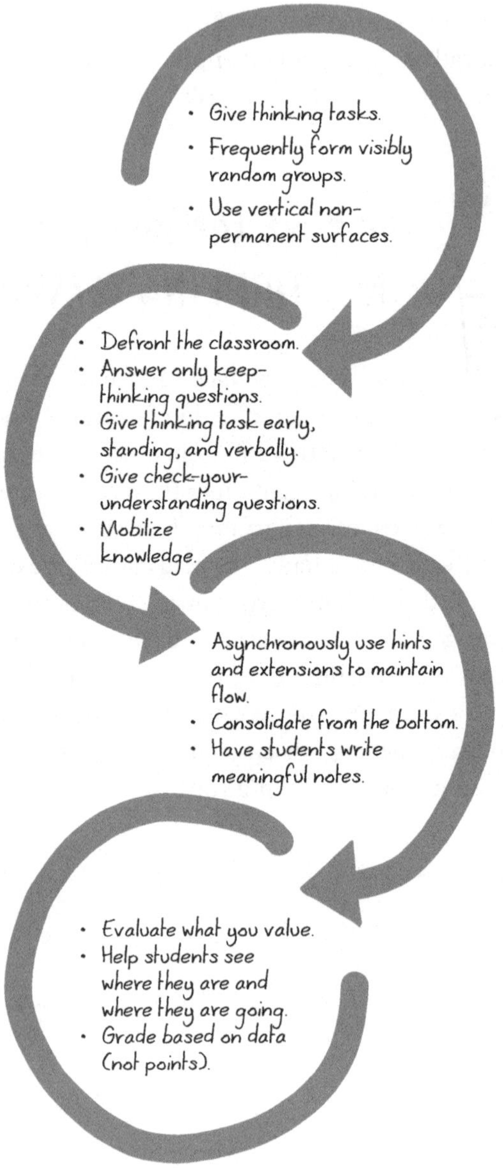

- Give thinking tasks.
- Frequently form visibly random groups.
- Use vertical non-permanent surfaces.

- Defront the classroom.
- Answer only keep-thinking questions.
- Give thinking task early, standing, and verbally.
- Give check-your-understanding questions.
- Mobilize knowledge.

- Asynchronously use hints and extensions to maintain flow.
- Consolidate from the bottom.
- Have students write meaningful notes.

- Evaluate what you value.
- Help students see where they are and where they are going.
- Grade based on data (not points).

Figure 3.1   Toolkits for Building a Thinking Classroom With Small Class Sizes

CATEGORY 2

VIRTUAL LEARNING ENVIRONMENTS

4

BUILDING A THINKING CLASSROOM FOR A SYNCHRONOUS VIRTUAL SETTING

. . . .

Virtual (or online) math courses have been with us long before the COVID-19 pandemic and will continue to be with us long after. In some cases, all or parts of these courses are synchronous—meaning that the students and teachers meet regularly through some sort of digital medium (Zoom, Microsoft Teams, Google Meets, etc.). It is still possible to build a thinking classroom in these synchronous virtual settings, but it will necessitate a slight adaptation of nine of the 14 thinking classroom practices. It will also require the introduction and use of a knowledgefeed as described in the introduction.

HOW GROUPS ARE FORMED IN A THINKING CLASSROOM

Practice 2

In a thinking classroom, we need to give students collaborators with whom to think. The best way to do this is through frequent and visibly random groupings. In face-to-face settings, the research shows that the ideal group size is three. With groups of three, there is a perfect balance between redundancy (the things individuals in a group have in common) and diversity (the unique things that every group member brings to the group).

When we form random groups of three students in a virtual setting, however, students can choose to not turn on their camera or their microphone, they may have technical difficulties with these devices, or there could be internet interruptions—all of which serve to reduce the diversity available to a group. Virtual environments are diversity-depleting spaces. So, we need to compensate for this—at least, at first. To ensure there is enough diversity in a group, we start building thinking classrooms in these virtual settings with groups of five students. As the proficiency with technology increases and the collaborative norms get established (see Practice 12), you can begin to reduce the group size back to three.

WHERE STUDENTS WORK IN A THINKING CLASSROOM

Practice 3

Once in their groups, students will need a work surface to show their shared thinking. In synchronous virtual settings, this is achieved through the use of a cloud-based digital whiteboard. Any collaborative software you are using (Zoom, Teams, Meet, etc.) likely has a digital whiteboard built in. The problem is that you, as the teacher, can usually not see these unless you join the group. This makes it more difficult to monitor progress among all the groups quickly. For this reason, I recommend using a third-party digital whiteboard that lives outside of your collaborative software.

There are several available for free and they are not hard to find, but the one that I have found works best is Jamboard. Jamboard is and always will be free—which is not always true of other products. It allows students to draw with a stylus or a mouse, add text boxes or sticky notes, add images, and erase. It even allows for students to use text boxes, sticky notes, and images as manipulatives. Finally, it allows all members of a group to work inside the same representational space at the same time, which nicely emulates the work at a vertical non-permanent surface (VNPS). The other nice feature is that if a group runs out of space, they can just add (or move to) another frame. Each Jamboard link can have up to 20 frames (see Figure 4.1).

Jamboard is a Google product and is purported to be able to handle 100 viewers at a time. This is true. However, it cannot handle 100 editors at one time. We have found that if you keep the number of editors to 15 or below, then the platform is very stable. So, you will need to create multiple Jamboard links and have a maximum of 15 students working on each link—whether in groups of five to begin or groups of three later on.

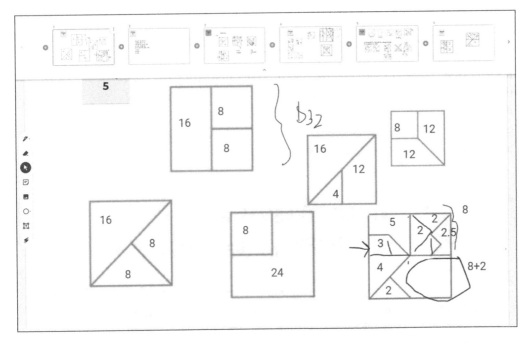

Figure 4.1 A Jamboard With Multiple Frames

Source: Created using Google Jamboard.

When students work on a VNPS, there is the restriction that there is only one whiteboard marker per group. Even in a socially distanced classroom where every student may have their own marker, there is only one student at the board at a time. These restrictions have been shown to enhance collaboration. The research showed that if every student had their own marker at a VNPS, then the group often degrades to three individuals working alongside each other. On Jamboard, every student has the ability to write at the same time. This is also true when they work on individual whiteboards. So, take extra care to establish appropriate collaborative behaviors in these settings (see Practice 12).

Practice 5

HOW WE ANSWER QUESTIONS IN A THINKING CLASSROOM

In many ways, answering questions in a synchronous virtual thinking classroom is the same as in a regular thinking classroom—you do not answer proximity and stop-thinking questions. But you have to be more vigilant about what students are asking, how to respond to the question, and what to do afterward. In a regular thinking classroom, if you get it wrong—mistake a keep-thinking question for a proximity question and smile and walk away—the student or group that asked the question can consult the other groups around them. If you have done a good job building the autonomy to access these resources, the number of questions (of any type) that you get decreases, and the need to respond to them correctly is less important. That is not true in a virtual thinking classroom. Although they can look at other groups' Jamboards, the inability for students to easily engage with other groups around their work is severely depleted. Students have access to fewer resources in these types of settings.

So, we have to get it more right. If you cannot decide if a question is a proximity question or a keep-thinking question, err on the side of keep-thinking and answer it. If you choose not to answer the question, circle back and try to see if the group is progressing despite you not answering their question. This is easier said than done. But there is a silver lining among all these restrictions and impediments—the knowledgefeed and the way it can be used to mobilize knowledge in these restricted thinking classrooms (see Practice 8). So, you may wish to direct them to scroll through the knowledgefeed looking for an answer to their question. And you may even choose to add something to the knowledgefeed for them to find. If you get asked the same question multiple times or anticipate needing to answer it multiple times, add an answer, in the form of a hint, to the knowledgefeed.

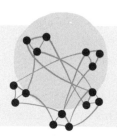

HOW WE FOSTER STUDENT AUTONOMY IN A THINKING CLASSROOM

Practice 8

The autonomy you want to foster in a thinking classroom is the autonomy to get knowledge from other groups—knowledge mobility. In a normal thinking classroom, students achieve this by passively glancing at other groups' vertical work and actively engaging other groups in discussion about their work. In a virtual synchronous thinking classroom, passive engagement is still possible through the use of the knowledgefeed, which creates a space that students can quickly glance at to gain a hint if they are stuck or an extension if they are ready to move on. Jamboards, with five groups to a single Jamboard, also offer the possibility for groups to passively glance at each other's work. To move this glancing beyond the specific Jamboard a group is working in, all the Jamboard links in use should be published on the knowledgefeed.

As we learned in the original research into building thinking classrooms, however, making the knowledge available is not enough—you need to help students access this knowledge. And as discussed in the anchor book, talking to students about this is not enough. You need to force them to access it by being deliberately less helpful. So, rather than answering their questions, direct them to a place in the knowledgefeed or Jamboards where they may find what they are looking for. This, coupled with specific attention to student behavior (see Practice 12), will increase knowledge mobility even in this synchronous virtual thinking classroom environment.

WHAT WE CHOOSE TO EVALUATE IN A THINKING CLASSROOM

Practice 12

The unique opportunities and restrictions created by the virtual synchronous environment require students to behave in specific ways for these thinking classroom adaptations to be effective. One of the best ways to shape these behaviors is to evaluate what you value. And what you should value in a synchronous virtual thinking classroom is that students are as attentive when the task is given out and when consolidation is going on as they would be if they were on their feet in an in-person thinking classroom. This means students have to be more responsible for their actions. To help with this, co-construct rubrics around what it means to be an engaged learner, or an attentive listener, or ready to learn. You can also build rubrics around what it means to gather ideas, what to do when stuck or finished, or how to be an effective group. This last rubric could also include language around how to take turns writing on the digital whiteboards. The focus on who is writing can also be in rubrics around collaboration, whiteboard etiquette, and so on. In short, just like in a normal thinking classroom, identify behaviors you would like to see changed and co-construct rubrics around these.

HOW WE ARRANGE THE FURNITURE (KNOWLEDGEFEED) IN A THINKING CLASSROOM

Practice 4

In a virtual synchronous classroom, there is no furniture with which to defront the classroom. But defronting the classroom is only a means to an end. And the end is to introduce enough chaos into the classroom that students perceive it as a safe place to think—to get messy and make mistakes. Defronting the classroom is only one way to achieve this. Just as when you're in a face-to-face classroom but limited to fixed seating in rows of desks, there are other ways to introduce small amounts of chaos. In any classroom that uses a knowledgefeed—whether it's face-to-face but socially distanced, hybrid, or virtual, the easiest way to do this is to allow the knowledgefeed to be messy. It is not critical to have all the information that gets posted on the knowledgefeed be organized—either thematically or chronologically. Thinking is messy and full of errors. Let the knowledgefeed display this. If you need to drop in a hint, don't obsess about putting it right next to the task it relates to or the question that prompted it. The same is true of screen captures or images that you and/or the students put into the knowledgefeed. In fact, while you don't want to be overly chaotic, make reasonable efforts to disrupt the logical and chronological flow of the knowledgefeed. Like student work, the knowledgefeed is an artifact of thinking, and it isn't always logical and orderly.

WHEN, WHERE, AND HOW TASKS ARE GIVEN IN A THINKING CLASSROOM

Practice 6

In a synchronous virtual thinking classroom, you still give tasks verbally in the first five minutes of class. However, you cannot give them with students standing around you, like in an in-person thinking classroom. In virtual environments, you need to pay extra attention to establishing norms around listening to the instructions in these settings (see Practice 12). Once you have given the task and the groups have started working, place the task on the knowledgefeed in a text-light form. That is, whereas the verbal instructions will contain elements of storytelling, narrative, and/or modeling, what you recorded is a simple set of instructions as to what the students are to do. For example, consider the unusual baker task from Chapter 9 of the anchor book. In the synchronous virtual setting, you may tell the story of the poor girl working in the bakery who has to figure out how big each piece is and how, as the day goes on, this becomes harder and harder for her to do. What you place on knowledgefeed, however, may be something like "Determine what fraction of a whole cake is for each of the following cakes."

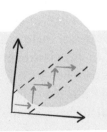

HOW WE USE HINTS AND EXTENSIONS IN A THINKING CLASSROOM

Practice 9

Even with students working in synchronous virtual environments, flow needs to be maintained, but it is much harder to get the timing right. In a normal thinking classroom, all the work that the groups are producing is visible at a glance. This allows a teacher to monitor progress and to interject hints and extensions when needed. Having students working in a virtual environment impedes our ability to quickly ascertain where groups are in their progress. So, the groups themselves have to use their ability to mobilize knowledge and maintain flow as they balance their ability and challenge. They need to seek out hints in the knowledgefeed or other Jamboards if they are stuck or find the next question on the knowledgefeed if they are ready to move on. Your job is still to create the flow sequence of tasks and to add these to the knowledgefeed, one at a time, in pace with the fastest moving groups. To be clear, this does not mean that you should simply post a list of questions on the knowledgefeed. The research clearly showed that this creates a reach-for-the-finish-line behavior that fractures collaboration. In order to maintain a focus on thinking while groups work on the task at hand, you need to distribute the flow sequence throughout the knowledgefeed among the various hints and images of groups' work.

HOW WE CONSOLIDATE A LESSON IN A THINKING CLASSROOM

Practice 10

In a normal thinking classroom, while students are working through the tasks you are giving out one at a time, you move around the room seeding ideas and locking in work in anticipation of the consolidation that will follow. In the virtual synchronous context, this still needs to happen. The difference is that locking in work is already occurring in the form of pictures and screen captures that are being posted to the knowledgefeed—whether by you or by students. As such, the gallery walk will be a guided tour through the knowledgefeed. Like a normal thinking classroom, however, this does not mean that we should showcase all the work. Nor does it mean that we just move through the work linearly. Careful selection and sequencing are still needed to build a narrative that can move students through the various levels of complexity and nuances encountered in the lesson.

Knowing that the knowledgefeed will become the source for the consolidation will invariably begin to shape what it is you, as the teacher, choose to capture and display in the knowledgefeed. It may even begin to shape what students choose to add to the knowledgefeed. But do not allow this reality to overly control the way in which the knowledge emerges. There is still a need for the knowledgefeed to maintain a certain amount of chaos in order to send the message to the students that messiness and errors are part of thinking (see Practice 4).

TOOLKITS

In a virtual synchronous thinking classroom, all 14 practices are still relevant. Some can be executed as usual; others need adaptations. Also in need of adaptation are the orders with which these practices are implements and the toolkits into which they cluster (see Figure 4.2).

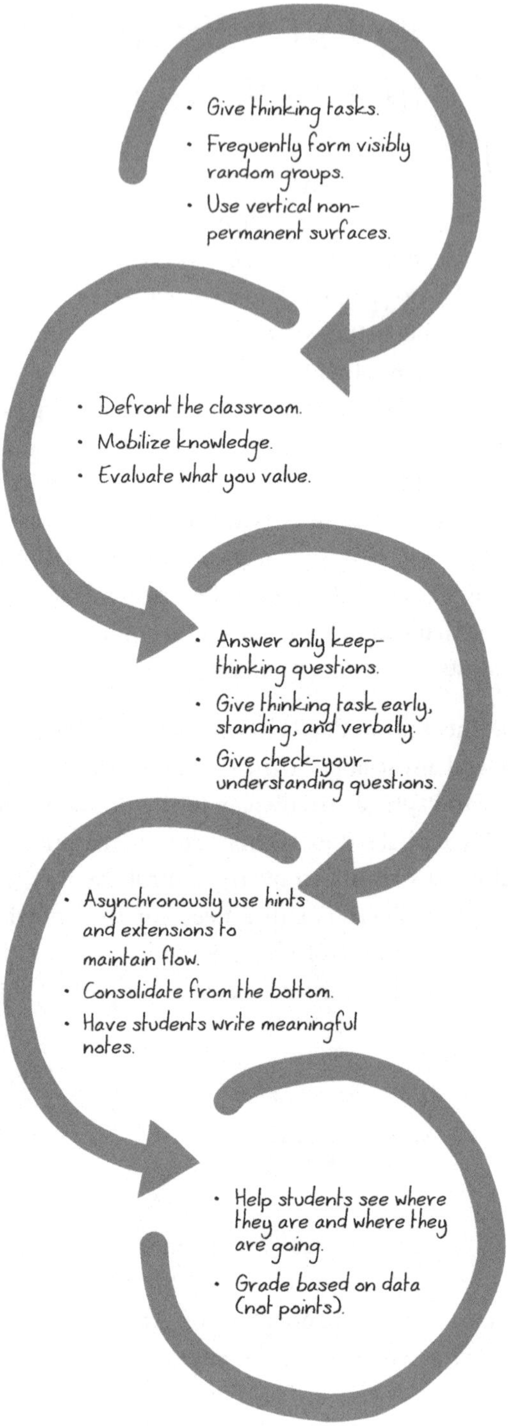

- Give thinking tasks.
- Frequently form visibly random groups.
- Use vertical non-permanent surfaces.

- Defront the classroom.
- Mobilize knowledge.
- Evaluate what you value.

- Answer only keep-thinking questions.
- Give thinking task early, standing, and verbally.
- Give check-your-understanding questions.

- Asynchronously use hints and extensions to maintain flow.
- Consolidate from the bottom.
- Have students write meaningful notes.

- Help students see where they are and where they are going.
- Grade based on data (not points).

Figure 4.2 Toolkits for Building a Thinking Classroom for Synchronous Virtual Setting

5

BUILDING A THINKING CLASSROOM IN AN ASYNCHRONOUS VIRTUAL SETTING

. . . .

Virtual (or online) math courses have been with us long before the COVID-19 pandemic and will continue to be with us long after. In some cases, all or parts of these courses are asynchronous—meaning that the students and teachers interact through mediums that are independent of time (email, chats, discussion boards, etc.). These courses are often built around a self-paced model of distance education wherein the students move independently through curricular content with intermittent access to the teacher through office hours. Even in these settings, it is still possible to build a thinking classroom as a thread that runs parallel to their independent curricular work. This will necessitate a slight adaptation of 10 of the 14 thinking classroom practices as well as the introduction of a knowledgefeed as described in the introduction. The remaining four practices (7, 11, 13, and 14) can be implemented, as described in the anchor book, to the independent curriculum work that the students do in these virtual asynchronous settings.

Practice 1

WHAT TYPES OF TASKS WE USE IN A THINKING CLASSROOM

If we want students to think, we have to give them something to think about. This is true no matter what setting you're in. In asynchronous virtual environments, you need to choose tasks that lend themselves to asynchronous discussions and take longer to solve. The tax collector (see Chapter 6 of the anchor book) is a great task for getting students to think. But it moves too quickly for an asynchronous environment. If one member of a group solves it in their first encounter and writes about the solution, there is not much for the rest of the group to do. Instead, we need to use tasks that take more time—more work. For example, consider the following problem:

> Pick three whole numbers at random—7, 12, and 5, for example. Below this string of numbers, write the sum of each adjacent pair. And below the list of sums, write the sum of adjacent pairs. And so on until there is only one number.

> The final number (36) is an even number. The question: Can we predict if the final number will be even or odd by only looking at the initial three numbers? What if there were four numbers to begin with? Five numbers? Six numbers? *N* numbers?

This task seems innocent enough. But solving it requires exploration, testing, the gathering of data, and a synthesis of these data into a hypothesis that, in turn, will need to be tested. What is interesting about this cycle is that regardless of how far a group gets with the task, at every stage they know more than they did previously, and they have some things that they can say about the answer. Whether they get all the way done or not, thinking and learning have happened. NRICH (https://nrich.maths.org/) has a rich source of tasks that can serve this purpose, as do the numeracy tasks (https://www.peterliljedahl.com/teachers/numeracy-tasks) mentioned in Chapter 1 of the anchor book.

Having said that, these tasks still need to provide easy access to all students while having enough evolving complexity to sustain a group's engagement for an extended period. The first such task that you use with your students should be non-curricular. After that, they should be focused on curricular content. For example, you can have students explore a series of functions and build conjectures as to how the various components of the functions will affect the graph of the function. You can have students engage in a project whereby they gather data on an event (like a candle burning) and organize, plot, and extrapolate these data to come to a conclusion. You will need to search for and develop these types of curricular tasks. The good news is, with the longer time dedicated to each such task, you will need fewer of them in a virtual asynchronous thinking classroom than you would in an in-person thinking classroom.

Practice 2

HOW GROUPS ARE FORMED IN A THINKING CLASSROOM

In a thinking classroom, we need to give students collaborators to think with. This is still true in an asynchronous virtual thinking classroom. As in face-to-face settings, you still want to form visibly random groups. In the asynchronous virtual setting, however, these groups will need to be larger than in face-to-face settings. The time lag students experience in asynchronous settings depresses the diversity that is in play at any one moment in the interaction between students in a group. Increasing the number of students in a group to four will increase the likelihood that new ideas are always in motion while at the same time not allowing for the creation of factions that we often see in larger groups. If you do not have a multiple of four students, use groups of three to assign the remainder—five is too many and two is too few.

Once formed, these groups will work asynchronously on the tasks at hand. Groups may choose, in addition to working asynchronously, to coordinate their own synchronous encounters through any one of a variety of mediums from a simple phone call or text message to FaceTime, Zoom, Google Meets, WhatsApp, and so on. Keeping the group size to four (or three) will make it easier to coordinate such encounters should the students wish to do so.

Given that these tasks take longer will mean, by necessity, that the students stay in these groups for longer than in a face-to-face setting. In the asynchronous settings, groups stay together for the length of a single task before being re-randomized.

WHERE STUDENTS WORK IN A THINKING CLASSROOM

Practice 3

Once in their groups, students will need to have access to an asynchronous work surface where they can share their individual thinking as well as show their shared thinking. In asynchronous virtual settings, this is best achieved through the use of a cloud-based digital whiteboard. There are several available for free and they are not hard to find, but the one that I have found works best for this kind of work is Jamboard. Jamboard is and always will be free—which is not always true of other products. It allows students to draw with a stylus or a mouse, add text boxes or sticky notes, add images, and erase. It even allows for students to use text boxes, sticky notes, and images as manipulatives (see Figure 5.1). Finally, it allows all members of a group to both synchronously and asynchronously work inside the same representational space. The other nice feature is that if a group or an individual runs out of space, they can just add (or move to) another frame. Each Jamboard link can have up to 20 frames (see Figure 5.1).

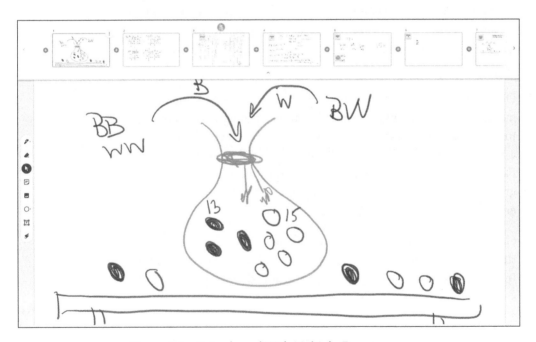

Figure 5.1 A Jamboard With Multiple Frames

Source: Created using Google Jamboard.

Given the length of time they work on a task, coupled with the exploratory nature of the tasks, I suggest that each group is given their own Jamboard to work on. This will give each group access to up to 20 frames of workspace. This may still not be enough workspace, so I further suggest that students be encouraged to create more Jamboards for themselves as needed.

Given that these groups will spend much of their time working asynchronously, the Jamboard may not be the only place individual students choose to work. They may want to work in a notebook or on a whiteboard. This is their choice, and this should be valued. However, at some point, the work they do will still need to be shared. Students can take pictures of their work and upload them to Jamboard or whatever platform they negotiate among themselves as the space where they wish to archive and share their individual work. This is discussed more in Practice 12.

Practice 5

HOW WE ANSWER QUESTIONS IN A THINKING CLASSROOM

In asynchronous virtual thinking classrooms, you should encourage students to pose their questions on the knowledgefeed. This will make the question and answer visible to all students and will help with the mobility of knowledge (see Practice 8). How you respond to these questions is, in many ways, the same as in a regular thinking classroom—do not answer questions that will cause the students to stop thinking. The difference is that there are no proximity questions. This means that you only have to distinguish stop-thinking questions from keep-thinking questions. In doing so, you have to be more vigilant about what students are asking, how to respond to the question, and what to do afterward. In a regular thinking classroom, if you get it wrong—for example, mistake a keep-thinking question for a stop-thinking question and smile and walk away—the student or group that asked the question can consult the other groups around them. If you have done a good job building the autonomy to access these resources, the number of questions (of any type) that you get decreases, and the need to respond to them correctly is less important. That is not true in a virtual asynchronous thinking classroom. Even though they can look at other groups' Jamboards, the inability for students to easily engage with other groups around their work is severely depleted. Students have access to fewer resources in these types of settings.

So, we have to get it more right. If you cannot decide if a question is a keep-thinking question, err on the side of keep-thinking and answer it. If you choose not to answer the question, drop a hint about where they might look to find the answer (a specific Jamboard frame, a specific group, or in an accessible resource like a textbook). This is easier said than done. But there is a silver lining among all these restrictions and impediments—the knowledgefeed and the way it can be used to mobilize knowledge in these restricted thinking classrooms (see Practice 8). So, you may wish to direct them to scroll through the knowledgefeed looking for an answer to their question. And you may even choose to add something to the knowledgefeed for them to find.

WHEN, WHERE, AND HOW TASKS ARE GIVEN IN A THINKING CLASSROOM

Practice 6

In an asynchronous virtual thinking classroom, you cannot give the task while students stand around you, like in an in-person thinking classroom. And the impact of what happens in the first five minutes of class loses all its meaning. However, you can still make a thinking task the first thing they engage with in the course or at the start of a particular unit. And you can still give the tasks verbally, in the form of a video wherein you vocalize the tasks as you model aspects of it on a digital whiteboard. For example, consider the task in Practice 1 of this chapter. You could record yourself playing out the following script:

Teacher: Consider a random list of three whole numbers.

[writes 7, 12, and 5 on a digital whiteboard]

Teacher: Now, I take the sum of adjacent numbers in this list.

[writes 19 and 17 underneath the original list]

Teacher: And I keep doing this—taking the sum of adjacent numbers—until I have just one number left.

[writes 36 under the previous line]

Teacher: This final number is even. Is there a way for us to predict if a particular list of three whole numbers will produce an even or an odd number in the end? What if we started with four numbers? Five numbers? And so on.

This video can be something the students can access over and over again if they need to hear or see more details of the task. This does not prevent you from also placing a text-light version of the task on the knowledgefeed. That is, whereas the verbal instructions will contain elements of storytelling, narrative, and/or modeling, what you place on the knowledgefeed is a simple set of instructions as to what the students are to do. For example, for the aforementioned problem, you may wish to simply put a screen capture from the video showing the inverted triangle of numbers and the text "Is there a way for us to predict if a particular list of three whole numbers will produce an even or an odd number in the end? What if we started with four numbers? Five numbers? N numbers?"

HOW WE ARRANGE THE FURNITURE (KNOWLEDGEFEED) IN A THINKING CLASSROOM

Practice 4

In a virtual asynchronous environment, there is no furniture with which to defront the classroom. But defronting the classroom is only a means to an end. And the end is to introduce enough chaos into the classroom that students perceive it as a safe place to think—to get messy and make mistakes. Defronting the classroom is only one way to achieve this. There are other ways to introduce small amounts of chaos. In a classroom that uses a knowledge feed, the easiest way to do this is to allow the knowledgefeed (see introduction) to be messy. Do not obsess over having all the information that gets posted on the knowledgefeed be thematically or chronologically organized. If you need to drop in a hint, it doesn't have to come right after the task it relates to. The same is true of screen captures or images that you and/or the students put into the knowledgefeed. Make efforts to deliberately disrupt the logical and chronological flow of it. The knowledgefeed, like student work, is an artifact of thinking. Thinking is messy and full of errors. Let the knowledgefeed display this. This is not to say that, like a classroom, it needs to be overly chaotic. Keep it reasonable. The students will be fine with this as they navigate numerous social media applications that defy logical organization.

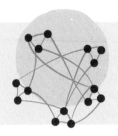

HOW WE FOSTER STUDENT AUTONOMY IN A THINKING CLASSROOM

Practice 8

The autonomy you want to foster in a thinking classroom is the autonomy to get knowledge from other groups—knowledge mobility. In a normal thinking classroom, students achieve this by passively glancing at other groups' vertical work and actively engaging other groups in discussion about their work. In a virtual asynchronous thinking classroom, passive engagement is still possible through the use of the knowledgefeed which creates a space that students can quickly glance at to gain a hint if they are stuck or an extension if they are ready to move on. Jamboards, or other digital whiteboards, also offer the possibility for groups to passively glance at each other's work. To move this glancing beyond the specific Jamboard a group is working in, all the Jamboard links in use should be published on the knowledgefeed, and students who create additional links should be encouraged to add these to the knowledgefeed.

As we learned in the original research into building thinking classrooms, however, making the knowledge available is not enough—you need to help students access this knowledge. And as discussed in the anchor book, talking to students about this is not enough. You need to force them to access it by being deliberately less helpful. So, rather than answering their questions, direct them to a place in the knowledgefeed or Jamboards where they may find what they are looking for. This, coupled with specific attention to student behavior (see Practice 12), will increase knowledge mobility even in this asynchronous virtual thinking classroom environment.

WHAT WE CHOOSE TO EVALUATE IN A THINKING CLASSROOM

Practice 12

The unique opportunities and restrictions created by the virtual asynchronous environment require students to behave in specific ways in order for these thinking classroom adaptations to be effective. One of the best ways to shape these behaviors is to evaluate what you value. And what you should value in an asynchronous virtual thinking classroom is that students work well together in their groups and that they access the resources available to them. To help with the first of these, co-construct rubrics around collaboration or group work. For the second, you can co-construct rubrics around what it means to gather ideas or what to do when stuck. In short, just like in a normal thinking classroom, identify behaviors you would like to see changed and co-construct rubrics around these.

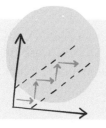

HOW WE USE HINTS AND EXTENSIONS IN A THINKING CLASSROOM

Practice 9

Even with students working in asynchronous virtual environments, you need to maintain flow, but it is much harder to get the timing right. In a normal thinking classroom, all the work that the groups are producing is visible at a glance. This allows a teacher to monitor progress and to interject hints and extensions when needed. Having students working virtually and asynchronously impedes our ability to quickly ascertain where groups are in their progress. So, the groups themselves have to use their ability to mobilize knowledge and maintain flow as they balance their ability and challenge. They need to seek out hints in the knowledgefeed or other Jamboards if they are stuck or find the next question or extension on the knowledgefeed if they are ready to move on. Your job is still to create the flow sequence of extensions and to add these to the knowledgefeed, one at a time, in pace with the fastest moving groups.

HOW WE CONSOLIDATE A LESSON IN A THINKING CLASSROOM

Practice 10

In a normal thinking classroom, while students are working through the tasks you are giving out one at a time, you move around the room seeding ideas and locking in work in anticipation of the consolidation that will follow. In the virtual asynchronous context, this still needs to happen. Some of this is already occurring in the form of pictures and screen captures that are being posted to the knowledgefeed—whether by the teacher or by students. What is missing is a coherent narrative that can take students through the work on the knowledgefeed. Your job, as a teacher in this setting, will be to build a cohesive narrative out of the work that can act as consolidation from the bottom. In doing so, keep in mind that you want to focus this narrative on reinforcing the foundational ideas rather than dwelling on the most sophisticated solutions that groups came up with. You can build this narrative by populating a PDF with images of student work and annotating it with your comments. Alternatively, you can record yourself flipping through images of student work as you mark up and annotate the work. I find that this recording is most easily done in Zoom while screen sharing a Jamboard that displays different student work on different frames. This way I can flip through the frames one at a time while drawing and writing on the work with either a red pen or the laser pointer built into the software.

Knowing that the knowledgefeed will become the source for the consolidation will invariably begin to shape what it is you, as the teacher, choose to capture and display in the knowledgefeed. It may even begin to shape what students choose to add to the knowledgefeed. But do not allow this reality to overly control the way in which the knowledge emerges. There is still a need for the knowledgefeed to maintain a certain amount of chaos in order to send the message to the students that messiness and errors are part of thinking (see Practice 4). You don't want them anticipating what you'll choose and thus limiting what they post, as that will shut the thinking down.

TOOLKITS

In a virtual asynchronous thinking classroom, all 14 practices are still relevant. Practices 7, 11, 13, and 14 can be executed as described in the anchor book within the independent curriculum work and would be hard-wired into the structure of that component of the course. The ones that apply to the thinking classroom thread will need adaptations. Also in need of adaptation are the orders with which these practices are implemented and the toolkits into which they cluster (see Figure 5.2).

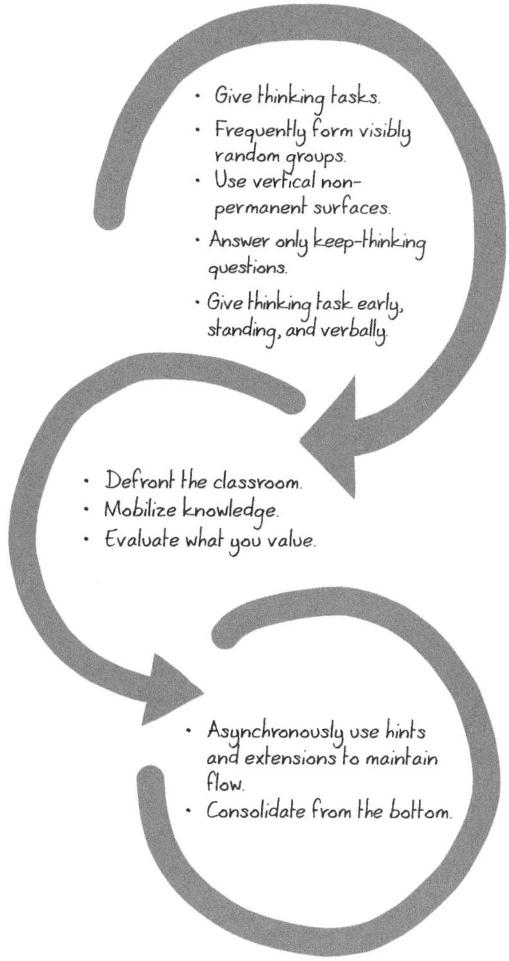

- Give thinking tasks.
- Frequently form visibly random groups.
- Use vertical non-permanent surfaces.
- Answer only keep-thinking questions.
- Give thinking task early, standing, and verbally.

- Defront the classroom.
- Mobilize knowledge.
- Evaluate what you value.

- Asynchronously use hints and extensions to maintain flow.
- Consolidate from the bottom.

Figure 5.2 Toolkits for Building a Thinking Classroom in an Asynchronous Virtual Setting

CATEGORY 3

HYBRID LEARNING ENVIRONMENTS

6

BUILDING A THINKING CLASSROOM FOR AN ASYNCHRONOUS HYBRID SETTING

. . . .

Prompted by the COVID-19 pandemic, and with the need for social distancing, many jurisdictions moved to hybrid models of teaching as a way to reduce the number of students in the room at any one time. There are several ways this is achieved, often by splitting a class into two groups—let's call them A and B—which are in-person some of the time and working at home some of the time. Here are a few common patterns:

- **Alternating Days.** Students in group A might come to school on Monday, Wednesday, Friday for synchronous in-person learning while working at home on Tuesday and Thursday. Group B would do the opposite, coming to school on Tuesday and Thursday for in-person learning while working independently at home on the other days. The following week this would switch with group B having Monday, Wednesday, and Friday as their in-days.

- **Longer Alternating Intervals.** In some cases, the intervals could be longer with students having two or more days in a row of in-person learning followed by the same number of days learning from home.

- **Shorter Alternating Intervals.** In some cases, particularly for elementary students, these intervals are shorter, with group A attending in-person in the morning and working at home in the afternoon, and group B working at home in the morning and attending in-person in the afternoon.

- **Common Home Time.** In other cases, the students are working in one of the aforementioned intervals, but there are one or more days a week where all the students work from home. For example, group A comes to school on Mondays and Wednesdays, while group B works from home on those days. On Tuesdays and Thursdays, group B is in school while group A is at home. And then all students work from home on Fridays. There are other variants as well, where there are days and times where all students are working at home.

In this chapter, I am going to discuss the situation where the students spend their out-of-class time doing asynchronous and independent work. I have seen this asynchronous hybrid model enacted in two different ways. The first of these is built on the idea that advancement through curriculum is achieved both during in-person time and home time. For example, group A might learn concepts 1, 2, 3 in class on Monday. They are then expected to learn concepts 4 and 5 on their own at home on Tuesday. The teacher would then continue with concepts 6, 7, and 8 in class on Wednesday and so on. Meanwhile, where group B learns these same concepts on days opposite to group A (see Figure 6.1).

Group A	1, 2, 3	4, 5	6, 7, 8	9	10, 11
Group B	1, 2, 3	4, 5	6, 7, 8	9	10, 11

Figure 6.1 Concept Distribution for Each Group

Note: White is at home and gray is in school.

Based on what I have observed about the thinking and learning in this model, I do not recommend it. Operating on the assumption that students will have learned concepts 4 and 5 at home on their own so that you can move on as a group to concepts 6, 7, and 8 is fraught with student stress and teacher frustration. Invariably, this results in teachers reducing the number of concepts students are expected to learn on their own, and/or teachers overlapping concepts learned at home with concepts covered in class. This continues until you inevitably get to a point where every concept is covered in class (see Figure 6.2)—albeit after the students have struggled to learn it on their own at home. This struggle does not mitigate student frustration, and the eventual realization that "the teacher is just going to do it in class anyway" often leads to students waiting for class to learn the concepts.

Group A	1, 2, 3	4, 5	4, 5, 6	7, 8	7, 8, 9
Group B	1, 2	1, 2, 3	4, 5	4, 5, 6	7, 8

Figure 6.2 Modified Concept Distribution for Each Group

Note: White is at home and gray is in school.

With this inevitability in mind, a better hybrid model, and the one I discuss in this chapter, is one where students' first exposure to concepts happens in the classroom and then they review and reify these concepts on their own at home (see Figure 6.3).

Group A	1, 2, 3	1, 2, 3	4, 5, 6	4, 5, 6	7, 8, 9
Group B		1, 2, 3	1, 2, 3	4, 5, 6	4, 5, 6

Figure 6.3 Reviewing and Reifying Concepts at Home

Note: White is at home and gray is in school.

In this model, you would build a thinking classroom as described in the anchor book for in-person learning—with some modification. In-class time would now be entirely dedicated to having students working through flow-sequenced curricular thinking tasks in their visibly random groups, on vertical non-permanent surfaces (VNPSs) followed by a carefully designed consolidation from the bottom—along with the rest of the practices that support these activities. The reifying activities of having students do check-your-understanding questions, making meaningful notes, and doing formative assessment are what students do at home.

This splitting of the thinking classroom practices into practices for the classroom and practices for home will require a slight modification to six of the thinking classroom practices. It will also require you to implement two knowledgefeeds. The first will be a *Q&A feed* where students post questions that you and other students can respond to. This question-and-answer feed should be the same for the entire unit of study (conics, algebra, trigonometry, fractions, etc.). The second knowledgefeed will be a *consolidation feed,* which will be used as a place to archive pictures from your in-class consolidation. There will be a unique consolidation feed for each lesson.

HOW WE ANSWER QUESTIONS IN A THINKING CLASSROOM

Practice 5

With the students that are in your classroom, you would answer (or not answer) questions exactly as you would in a normal thinking classroom (see the anchor book). But, the students who are working asynchronously at home may also have questions. If they do, they should be encouraged to pose their questions on the Q&A feed. Both the students and the teacher can capture images from in-class VNPS work and post them to the Q&A feed either in response to a question or as important information to archive. Using a knowledgefeed, as opposed to a discussion board, to host the Q&A feed works better because of the ease with which you or the students can drop in images of student work. The students will need some encouragement to autonomously post and respond to questions on this resource (see Practice 8).

But, like in a face-to-face setting, be aware of what type of question is being asked and how you respond to them. The difference is that in the Q&A feed there are no proximity questions. This means that you only have to distinguish stop-thinking questions from keep-thinking questions. In doing so, you have to be more vigilant about what students are asking, how to respond to the question, and what to do afterward. In a regular thinking classroom, if you get it wrong—mistake a keep-thinking question for a stop-thinking question and smile and walk away—the student or group who asked the question can consult the other groups around them. If you have done a good job building the autonomy to access these resources, the number of questions (of any type) that you get decreases, and the need to respond to them correctly is less important. That is not true for students working on their own at home. These students have access to fewer resources.

So, we have to get it more right. If you cannot decide if a question is a keep-thinking question, err on the side of keep-thinking and answer it. If you choose not to answer the question, drop a hint about where on the knowledgefeed they might look to find the answer. And you may even choose to add something to the knowledgefeed for them to find.

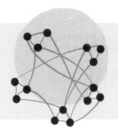

HOW WE FOSTER STUDENT AUTONOMY IN A THINKING CLASSROOM

Practice 8

Creating and using this Q&A feed as described will make knowledge accessible to students when they are working on their own at home. But, as we learned in the original research into building thinking classrooms, making the knowledge available is not enough—you need to help students to access this knowledge. And as discussed in the anchor book, talking to students about this is also not enough. You need to force them to access it by being deliberately less helpful. So, rather than answering their questions, direct them to a place in the knowledgefeed where they may find what they are looking for. This, coupled with specific attention to student behavior (see Practice 12), will increase knowledge mobility even in this asynchronous hybrid thinking classroom environment.

WHAT WE CHOOSE TO EVALUATE IN A THINKING CLASSROOM

Practice 12

The asynchronous hybrid setting, like all the settings in this supplement, will require students to behave in specific ways in order for the aforementioned adaptation to the thinking classroom practices to be effective. One of the best ways to shape these behaviors is to evaluate what you value. And what you should value in this setting is that students develop the skills to access resources when they are working from home. To show them that you value these skills, co-construct rubrics with them around what it means to pose questions to the Q&A feed, seek out answers on the Q&A feed, and use the consolidation feed as a resource when making meaningful notes. In short, just like in a conventional thinking classroom, identify behaviors you would like to see changed and co-construct rubrics around these.

HOW WE ARRANGE THE FURNITURE (KNOWLEDGEFEED) IN A THINKING CLASSROOM

Practice 4

For the in-class students, the room still needs to be defronted. For the students working at home, however, there is no classroom to defront. But defronting the classroom is only a means to an end. And the end is to introduce enough chaos into the classroom that students perceive that it is a safe place to get messy and make mistakes—and to think. Defronting the classroom is only one way to achieve this. There are other ways to introduce small amounts of chaos.

For students working asynchronously at home, this chaos can occur on the Q&A feed. The easiest way to do this is to allow this feed to be messy. Do not obsess over having all the questions and answers that get posted on the knowledgefeed be thematically or chronologically organized. If you need to drop in a hint, it doesn't have to come right after a specific question. Make efforts to deliberately disrupt the logical and chronological flow of it. The Q&A feed, like student work, is an artifact of thinking. Thinking is messy and full of errors. Let the Q&A feed display this as well.

HOW WE CONSOLIDATE A LESSON IN A THINKING CLASSROOM

Practice 10

Consolidation in an asynchronous hybrid setting is done in the same way as described in the anchor book. Whereas in a face-to-face setting consolidation can be delayed to the next lesson, in the asynchronous hybrid setting it must be done at the end of every lesson. And after it is done, you need to take pictures of the VNPSs that you used in the gallery walk and post them, in order, to the consolidation feed. You will need one of these feeds for every unit of study, and you will want to demarcate one lesson from the next. You are running each lesson twice—one for group A and one for group B—and even though there may be a lot of redundancy between these two lessons, post the pictures from each consolidation on the feed. The students should have access to the images that correspond to their memories of the lesson.

Practice 11

HOW STUDENTS TAKE NOTES IN A THINKING CLASSROOM

As mentioned in the introduction to this chapter, meaningful notes are something students will now do at home. The *consolidation feed* will help with this.

TOOLKITS

In a setting where your students alternate between working in class and working asynchronously at home, all 14 practices are still relevant. Some can be executed as usual; others need adaptations. Also in need of adaptation are the orders with which these practices are implemented and the toolkits into which they cluster (see Figure 6.4).

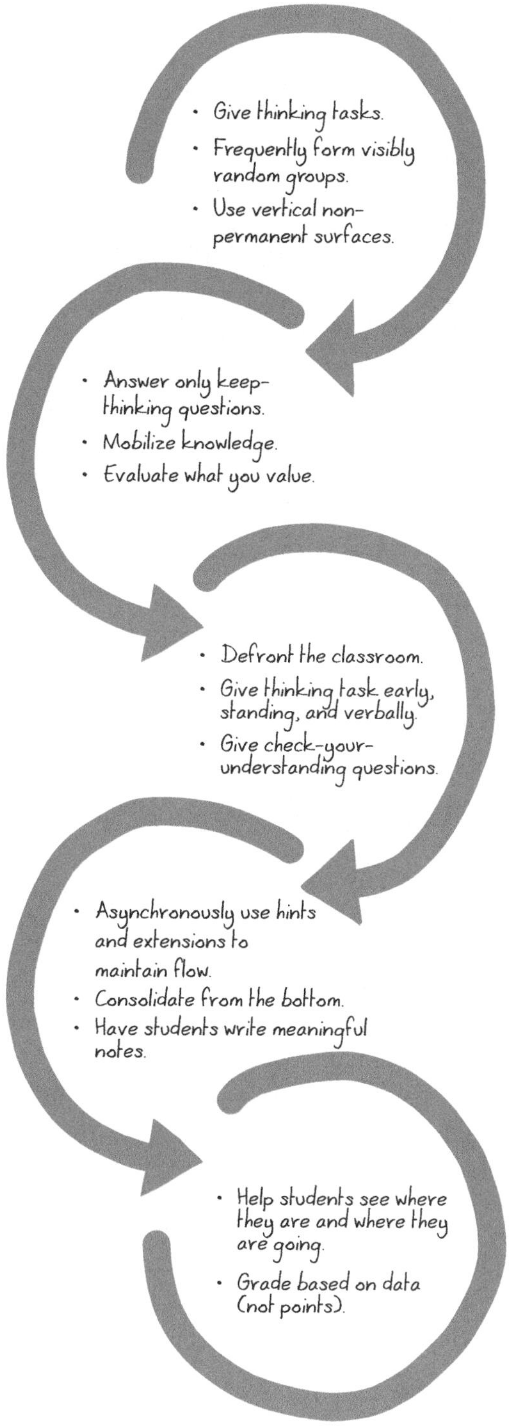

- Give thinking tasks.
- Frequently form visibly random groups.
- Use vertical non-permanent surfaces.

- Answer only keep-thinking questions.
- Mobilize knowledge.
- Evaluate what you value.

- Defront the classroom.
- Give thinking task early, standing, and verbally.
- Give check-your-understanding questions.

- Asynchronously use hints and extensions to maintain flow.
- Consolidate from the bottom.
- Have students write meaningful notes.

- Help students see where they are and where they are going.
- Grade based on data (not points).

Figure 6.4 Toolkits for Building a Thinking Classroom for an Asynchronous Hybrid Setting

7

BUILDING A THINKING CLASSROOM FOR A SYNCHRONOUS HYBRID SETTING

· ·

During the COVID-19 pandemic, many jurisdictions moved to hybrid models of teaching as a way to reduce the number of students in the classroom at any one time. There are several ways this is achieved, often by splitting a class into two groups—let's call them A and B—which are in person at some times and working at home at other times. As mentioned in Chapter 6, the four most common ways to enact this are the following:

- **Alternating Days.** Students in group A might come to school on Monday, Wednesday, Friday for synchronous in-person learning while working at home on Tuesday and Thursday. Group B would do the opposite, coming to school on Tuesday and Thursday for in-person learning while working independently at home on the other days. The following week this would switch with group B having Monday, Wednesday, and Friday as their in-days.

- **Longer Alternating Intervals.** In some cases, the intervals of in/out days could be longer with students having two or more days in a row of in-person learning followed by the same number of days learning from home.

- **Shorter Alternating Intervals.** In some cases, particularly for elementary students, these intervals shorter, with group A attending in-person in the morning and working at home in the afternoon, and group B working at home in the morning and attending in-person in the afternoon.

- **Common Home Time.** In other cases, the students are working in one of the aforementioned intervals, but there are one or more days a week where all the students work from home. For example, group A comes to school on Mondays and Wednesdays while group B works from home on those days. On Tuesdays and Thursdays, group B is in school while group A is at home. And then all students work from home on Fridays. There are other variants as well, where there are days and times where all students are working at home.

Another way that synchronous hybrid settings are being enacted is where there is little or no switching between school and home—the students who are learning in school are always learning in school and the students who are working from home are always, or mostly, working from home. This scenario is most often enacted in settings where there are a small number of students who, for whatever reason, are not able to attend school but are still enrolled in your class.

In this chapter, I am going to discuss the situation where the students who are working at home are expected to be synchronously engaged with what is happening in class by joining the class through Zoom, Teams, Meets, and so on. This is, by far, the most challenging model of education in this supplement. It is incredibly taxing on the teacher to try to maintain a lesson for their face-to-face students while at the same time trying to attend to the students who are present virtually. Having said that, it is still possible to build a thinking classroom within these settings. To do so, however, will require the adaptation of 11 of the thinking classroom practices.

You will also need to enact and use a knowledgefeed as described in the introduction. There should be a single and unique knowledgefeed for each lesson. In this synchronous hybrid setting, this will be used primarily by the students working from home, but the knowledgefeed should be projected on the screen for the in-class students to see. In-class students should also have access to the link and be able to use it, and contribute to it, in the same way that the students working from home do.

HOW GROUPS ARE FORMED IN A THINKING CLASSROOM

Practice 2

In a thinking classroom, we need to give students collaborators to think with. This is still true in a synchronous hybrid thinking classroom. How you make these groupings will depend largely on how many students you have connecting virtually. If it is just one or two, then ensure that each student connecting virtually is on a unique portable device—tablet, laptop, phone—and make visibly random groups as described in the anchor book. The only restriction is that you need to ensure that no more than one virtually connecting student is in any one group. A group that is randomly assigned a virtually connecting student is then responsible for collecting the device that the student is connecting through, bringing it to their workspace, and engaging with the student as though they were physically present.

If there are a large number of students connecting virtually, then form random groups within each medium—face-to-face students are put into random groups with face-to-face students and virtually present students are put into random groups with other virtually present students. While in face-to-face settings, the research showed that the ideal group size was three (two for primary), which provides a perfect balance between redundancy (the things individuals in a group have in common) and diversity (the unique things that every group member brings to the group). It also helps the teacher ensure that all students in a group are active and engaged.

However, if the group is connecting virtually, we do not have that same level of control. Students who connect virtually can choose to not turn on their camera or their microphone, they may have technical difficulties with these devices, or there could be internet interruptions—all of which serve to reduce the diversity available to a group. So, to ensure that there is enough diversity in these virtual groups, we need to initially build our thinking classrooms with groups of five students. As the proficiency with technology increases and the collaborative norms get established (see Practice 12), you can begin to reduce the group size back to three.

WHERE STUDENTS WORK IN A THINKING CLASSROOM

Practice 3

Once in their groups, students will need a work surface to show their shared thinking. For the face-to-face groups or the face-to-face groups who have just one virtually connecting member, the work surface they will use is a vertical non-permanent surface (VNPS). The virtual groups, however, will need to use a cloud-based digital whiteboard. Whatever collaborative software you are using (Zoom, Teams, Meets, etc.) likely has a digital whiteboard built right in. The problem is that you, as the teacher, can usually not see these unless you join the group. This makes it more difficult to monitor progress among all the groups quickly. For this reason, I recommend using a third-party digital whiteboard that lives outside of your collaborative software.

There are several available for free and they are not hard to find, but the one that I have found works best is Jamboard. Jamboard is and always will be free—which is not always true of other products. It allows students to draw with a stylus or a mouse, add text boxes or sticky notes, add images, and erase. It even allows for students to use text boxes, sticky notes, and images as manipulatives. Finally, it allows all members of a group to work inside the same representational space at the same time, which nicely emulates the work at a VNPS. The other nice feature is that if a group runs out of space, they can just add (or move to) another frame. Each Jamboard link can have up to 20 frames (see Figure 7.1).

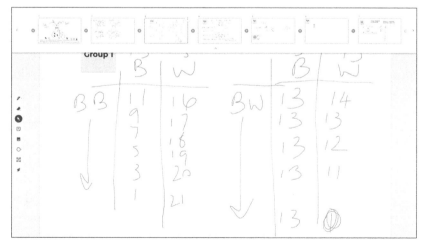

Figure 7.1 A Jamboard With Multiple Frames

Source: Created using Google Jamboard.

Jamboard is a Google product and, like other Google products, is purported to be able to handle 100 viewers at a time. This is true. However, if all those viewers also have editor privileges, then Jamboard gets buggy. I have found that if you keep the number of editors to 15 or below, then the platform is very stable. So, in the unlikely event that you have more than 15 students connecting virtually, you will need two (or more) Jamboard links and have a maximum of 15 students working on each link—whether in groups of five to begin with or groups of three later on.

When students work on a VNPS, there is the restriction that there is only one whiteboard marker per group. Even in a socially distanced classroom (see Chapter 1) where every student may have their own marker, there is only one student at the board at a time. These restrictions have been shown to enhance collaboration. On Jamboard, however, every student has the ability to write at the same time. So, take extra care to establish appropriate collaborative behaviors in these settings (see Practice 12).

HOW WE ANSWER QUESTIONS IN A THINKING CLASSROOM

Practice 5

With the students that are in your classroom, you would answer (or not answer) questions exactly as you would in any face-to-face thinking classroom (see the anchor book). The students who are working from home, however, should be encouraged to pose their questions on the knowledgefeed. This will make the question and answer visible to all students and will help with how students autonomously access additional resources and mobilize knowledge (see Practice 8) in this synchronous hybrid setting.

In a face-to-face thinking classroom, if your response to a question is to smile and walk away, the group that asked the question can consult the other groups around them. If you have done a good job building the autonomy to access these resources, the number of questions (of any type) that you get decreases, and the need to respond to them correctly is less important. That is not true for students working on their own at home as they have access to fewer resources. This means that you will need to be more aware of what types of questions are being asked and how you respond to them.

In the knowledgefeed, there are no proximity questions, but there are still stop-thinking questions and keep-thinking questions, and you will need to distinguish between these. If you cannot decide if a question is a keep-thinking question, err on the side of keep-thinking and answer it. If you choose not to answer the question, drop a hint about where on the knowledgefeed they might look to find the answer. And you may even choose to add something to the knowledgefeed for them to find.

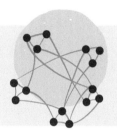

HOW WE FOSTER STUDENT AUTONOMY IN A THINKING CLASSROOM

Practice 8

Creating and using this knowledgefeed as described will make knowledge accessible to students when they are working in groups from home. But, as we learned in the original research into building thinking classrooms, making the knowledge available is not enough. You also have to help students access it. And as discussed in the anchor book, talking to students about this is not enough. You need to force them to access it by being deliberately less helpful. As discussed in Practice 5, rather than answering their questions, direct them to a place in the knowledgefeed where they may find it. This, coupled with specific attention to student behavior (see Practice 12), will increase knowledge mobility even in this synchronous hybrid thinking classroom environment.

WHAT WE CHOOSE TO EVALUATE IN A THINKING CLASSROOM

Practice 12

The synchronous hybrid setting, like all the settings in this supplement, will require students to behave in specific ways in order for the aforementioned adaptation to the thinking classroom practices to be effective. One of the best ways to shape these behaviors is to evaluate what you value. And what you should value in this setting is that students develop the skills to access resources when they are working from home. To show them that you value these skills co-construct rubrics with them around what it means to pose questions on the knowledgefeed, to seek out hints and extensions on the knowledgefeed, to contribute work and answers to the knowledgefeed, and to use the knowledgefeeds as a resource when making meaningful notes. In short, just like in a conventional thinking classroom, identify behaviors you would like to see changed and co-construct rubrics around these.

HOW WE ARRANGE THE FURNITURE (KNOWLEDGEFEED) IN A THINKING CLASSROOM

Practice 4

For the in-class students, the room still needs to be defronted. For the students connecting virtually, however, there is no furniture with which to defront the classroom. But defronting the classroom is only a means to an end. And the end is to introduce enough chaos into the classroom that students perceived it as a safe place to think—to get messy and make mistakes. Defronting the classroom is only one way to achieve this. There are other ways to introduce small amounts of chaos. For the students working from home, the easiest way to do this is to allow the knowledgefeed to be messy. Do not obsess over having all the information that gets posted on the knowledgefeed be thematically or chronologically organized. If you need to drop in a hint, it doesn't have to come right after the question that prompted it or the task it relates to. The same is true of screen captures or images that you and the students put into the knowledgefeed. Make efforts to deliberately disrupt the logical and chronological flow of it. The knowledgefeed, like student work, is an artifact of thinking. Thinking is messy and full of errors. Let the knowledgefeed also display this.

WHEN, WHERE, AND HOW TASKS ARE GIVEN IN A THINKING CLASSROOM

Practice 6

In a synchronous hybrid thinking classroom, you still give tasks verbally in the first five minutes of class. And you can still do so with the in-class students standing around you. But you need to ensure that the at-home students can see this delivery. The easiest way to do this is to connect to the collaborative platform (Zoom, Teams, Meet, etc.) from your phone (a tablet or laptop also works). Then simply have one of the in-class students *livestream* the delivery of the task to the collaborative platform using your phone.

Once you have given the task and the groups have started working, place the task on the knowledgefeed in a text-light form. That is, whereas the verbal instructions will contain elements of storytelling, narrative, and/or modeling, what you recorded is a simple set of instructions as to what the students are to do. For example, consider the wine chest problem in Chapter 5 of the anchor book. For the verbal delivery of the task, you may tell the story that accompanies the task. But what you post on the knowledgefeed may only be something like "If you will not drink wine that has been exposed to light more than 10 times, how often will you have to go to the wine store?"

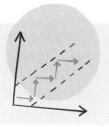

HOW WE USE HINTS AND EXTENSIONS IN A THINKING CLASSROOM

Practice 9

Even with students working in synchronous hybrid environments, flow needs to be maintained. For the students working in class, you do this as described in the anchor book. For these students, all the work that the groups are producing is visible at a glance. This allows you to monitor progress and to interject hints and extensions when needed. This is much more difficult for the students working in virtual groups. So, the groups have to self-manage much of the mobilization of knowledge and maintenance of flow by seeking out hints and extensions in the knowledgefeed or other Jamboards if they are stuck or by finding the next question on the knowledgefeed if they are ready to move on. Your job is still to create the flow sequence of tasks and to add these to the knowledgefeed, one at a time, in pace with the fastest moving virtual groups. To be clear, this does not mean that you should simply post a list of questions on the knowledgefeed. The research clearly showed that this creates a reach-for-the-finish-line behavior that fractures collaboration.

HOW WE CONSOLIDATE A LESSON IN A THINKING CLASSROOM

Practice 10

In a normal thinking classroom, while students are working through the tasks you are giving out one at a time, you move around the room seeding ideas and locking in work in anticipation of the consolidation that will follow. In the synchronous hybrid setting context, this still needs to happen. To make the job of consolidation easier, I suggest that you lead your gallery walk entirely through the VNPS work produced in class and have a student use your phone to livestream it for those working from home. After having done the consolidation go around and take pictures of each board that you visited during the consolidation and post these to the end of the knowledgefeed in the same order as happened in the consolidation.

Alternatively, you can take your students on a guided tour through the knowledgefeed. Like in a normal thinking classroom, however, this does not mean that we should showcase all the work. Nor does it mean that we just move through the work linearly. Careful selection and sequencing are still needed to build a narrative that can move students through the various levels of complexity and nuances encountered in the lesson. If you plan to use the knowledgefeed as the source for the consolidation, then you will need to begin to add images to it ahead of time. These images can be screen captures from the Jamboards or pictures of the VNPSs. This is not to say that these images should be placed in the knowledgefeed in a logical or chronological order. Order and logic will emerge out of the guided tour.

Finally, you may choose to use a combination of the VNPS work, the Jamboard work, and the knowledgefeed as the sources for your gallery walk. This can not only be challenging but also worthwhile as it demonstrates that all work is valuable, whether produced in class or from home. If this is the route you are going to take, I suggest that you capture the images from each stop on the gallery walk and post them, in order, to the end of the knowledgefeed.

HOW STUDENTS TAKE NOTES IN A THINKING CLASSROOM

Practice 11

Irrespective of how the consolidation is conducted, students will still need to make meaningful notes for themselves. In the case of a synchronous hybrid classroom, the images from the consolidation that are archived on the knowledgefeed will help students produce these notes.

TOOLKITS

In a setting where your students alternate between working in class and working at home, all 14 practices are still relevant. Some can be executed as usual; others need adaptations. Also in need of adaptation are the orders with which these practices are implemented and the toolkits into which they cluster (see Figure 7.2).

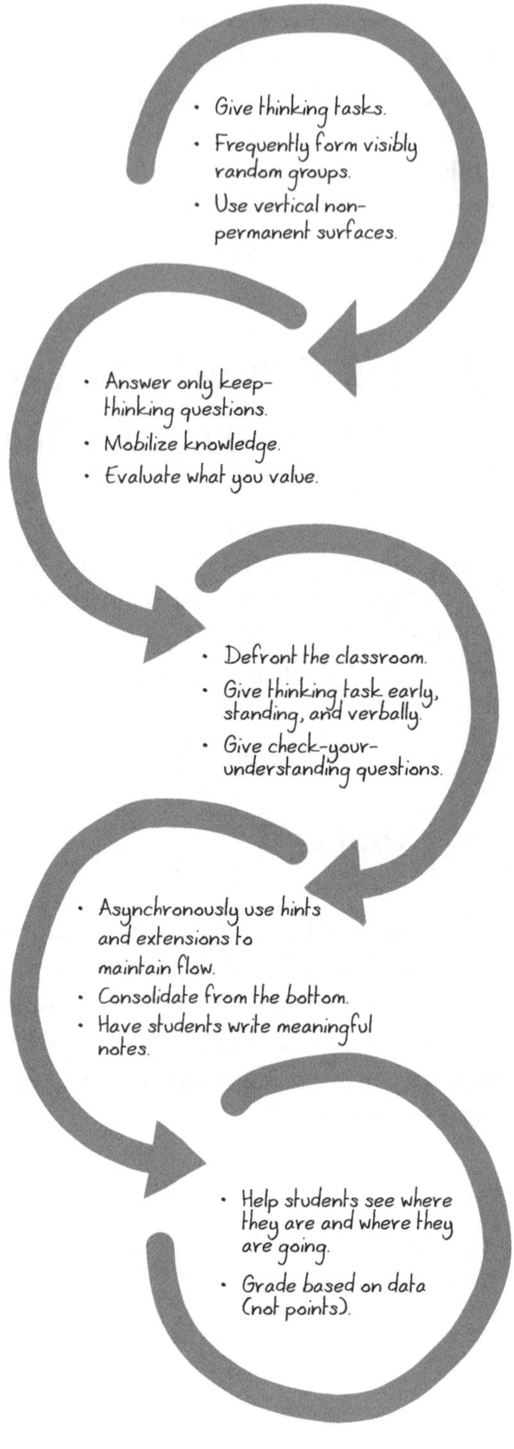

- Give thinking tasks.
- Frequently form visibly random groups.
- Use vertical non-permanent surfaces.

- Answer only keep-thinking questions.
- Mobilize knowledge.
- Evaluate what you value.

- Defront the classroom.
- Give thinking task early, standing, and verbally.
- Give check-your-understanding questions.

- Asynchronously use hints and extensions to maintain flow.
- Consolidate from the bottom.
- Have students write meaningful notes.

- Help students see where they are and where they are going.
- Grade based on data (not points).

Figure 7.2   Toolkits for Building a Thinking Classroom for a Synchronous Hybrid Setting

CATEGORY 4

OTHER LEARNING ENVIRONMENTS

8

BUILDING A THINKING CLASSROOM FOR INDEPENDENT LEARNING

. . . .

A setting that has existed in school systems for many years is independent learning, wherein students participate in a course as independent, self-paced learners. If this learning follows the old distance education model where students work entirely on their own with only occasional one-on-one interaction with a teacher, then there is not much that can be offered from the thinking classroom research beyond what was discussed in Chapter 5. If, however, this context involves some synchronous encounters where all the students enrolled in the course (or different courses) come together from time to time—either virtually or face-to-face—then all the thinking classroom practices are relevant with seven needing some adaptation to fit the context. This is true even if the students that are coming together are working on different courses and/or are in different places within their courses.

The intention of having students come together from time to time is often to create efficient opportunities for teachers to check in on progress and to create a space where students can seek help from the teacher. A portion of each session should still be devoted to this. But a portion of these synchronous encounters should also be used to develop a culture of thinking. If these encounters are virtual, refer to Chapter 4.

WHAT TYPES OF TASKS WE USE IN A THINKING CLASSROOM

Practice 1

To build a culture of thinking, we need to give students something to think about. This is true regardless of setting or context. Like other settings, building this culture is best achieved by beginning with highly engaging non-curricular tasks. Whereas other settings will then transition to using curricular tasks as thinking tasks, the transition from non-curricular to curricular tasks is a little different for independent self-paced learners. In this setting, every synchronous meeting with the students begins with them working on a highly engaging non-curricular task. This is then followed by having them work on a flow-sequenced series of curricular tasks (see Practice 9).

HOW GROUPS ARE FORMED IN A THINKING CLASSROOM

Practice 2

Even though these students are all working on different topics, different courses, and even at different grade levels, for the *non-curricular tasks* they are put into visibly random groups as they would be in a fully in-person thinking classroom setting. Such tasks transcend differences in prerequisite knowledge and allow for a thinking culture and community to be developed and sustained among these diverse learners.

For the flow-sequenced *curricular tasks*, however, they should work in self-selected affinity groups. These may be social in nature or organized around specific courses. The important thing is that they choose who they work with. Some may even choose to work alone. As time goes on and they have more and more experiences working in random groups on the non-curricular tasks, the community among these learners will strengthen, and you will see them begin to use each other as resources to help them with their individualized work.

We have seen this many times. Students working on very different curricular tasks, even from different courses or grades, begin to collaborate. Even though the students are working on different topics, there is knowledge in the room, and the random groups at the beginning of every session are helping this knowledge to begin to mobilize. This can be helped along by the teacher being deliberately less helpful (see Practice 8).

WHERE STUDENTS WORK IN A THINKING CLASSROOM

Practice 3

For their work on the non-curriculum tasks in random groups, they work at vertical non-permanent surfaces (VNPSs). For the flow-sequenced curricular tasks, they work where want—at their tables or at VNPSs. Over time, many will begin to gravitate to the VNPSs. You can influence this where you choose to engage learners that have questions. At its core, these synchronous sessions are meant to be open office hours where students can get help from their teacher. So, whether they need your help on a flow-sequenced curricular task or are seeking guidance on their self-paced learning, have them meet you at a VNPS. This will help promote the efficacy of these vertical spaces for thinking whether they are working together or alone.

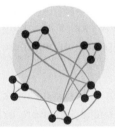

HOW WE FOSTER STUDENT AUTONOMY IN A THINKING CLASSROOM

Practice 8

In these groups of independent learners who are meeting, you do not want to be the only source of knowledge in the room. You will still want, as much as possible, to mobilize the knowledge in the room. Like other thinking classroom settings, you can achieve this by fostering the autonomy to seek out and access the knowledge possessed by other groups or individuals in the room. The challenge is that in a thinking classroom of independent self-paced learners, the knowledge that exists in the room is less visible to the students.

As a result, you act more like a switchboard, helping connect those who need particular knowledge with those who have it. So, rather than helping a student who has a question, direct them to a student or a group in the room who you know can help. If this student or group happens to be working at a VNPS, they will seem to be more approachable.

WHAT WE CHOOSE TO EVALUATE IN A THINKING CLASSROOM

Practice 12

This context, like all the contexts in this supplement, will require students to behave in specific ways in order for the aforementioned adaptations to the thinking classroom practices to be effective. One of the best ways to shape these behaviors is to evaluate what you value. And what you should value in a thinking classroom of independent self-paced learners is that students develop good collaboration skills. To show them that you value these qualities and that these qualities are valuable, co-construct rubrics with them around what it means to be a good group member, what good VNPS etiquette looks like, or what it means to be a good collaborator.

When in their groups, we need students and groups to access the resources around them by glancing at other groups' VNPSs. And the need to access these resources extends to when they are working independently on their flow-sequenced curricular tasks. Build rubrics around what it means to gather ideas or what to do when stuck or finished. In short, just like in a conventional thinking classroom, identify behaviors you would like to see changed and co-construct rubrics around these.

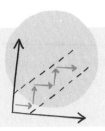

HOW WE USE HINTS AND EXTENSIONS IN A THINKING CLASSROOM

Practice 9

Whether students are working with their random groups on the non-curricular tasks or in self-selected groups on a sequence of curricular tasks, you still need to maintain flow. For the non-curricular tasks, the work of keeping groups in flow through hints and extensions is the same as in a face-to-face thinking classroom, as described in the anchor book. How you manage flow while the students are working on their own curricular tasks will be different, however.

It is one thing to maintain flow for 10 groups all working on the same sequence of tasks. It is quite another to do so for a class where each student is working on different topics. In such settings, you need to offload much of the work of managing hints and extensions onto the students. Unlike a conventional thinking classroom, where extensions are given out as groups are ready, in this setting you need to give each student a list of curricular tasks relevant to the topic they are currently on. To create and maintain flow, this list must be sequenced in such a way that each task is incrementally more challenging than the task that comes before it and is accompanied by a set of answers (not worked solutions) that students can use to autonomously get feedback on whether they are heading in the right direction. Having this list will allow students to autonomously increase the challenge of the task as their abilities increase, leaving you to provide hints as they get stuck and mobilize the knowledge that is already in the room.

Remember that providing students with these lists of flow-sequenced tasks was shown to be problematic in the fully in-person thinking classroom setting as it often changed the mindset of the students from thinking and learning in the moment to racing to get done. But when working with 10 to 30 independent self-paced learners, working across many different topics, there isn't much choice. Having said that, there are things you can do to keep the students in the moment and avoid the pitfalls of striving to be finished. First, make the lists of tasks *very* long. Long lists can be intimidating to students, in that they look like a lot of work. Ironically, *very* long lists are less intimidating in that they feel like an *impossible* amount of work. Couple this with the ongoing discourse that they are not expected to finish and what is important is that they understand and learn from whatever task they are currently working on. You might liken it to a puzzle or video game that has endless levels, and as you complete one, there's just one more, so there's never really a "done." At the same time, you can include the need to be in the moment on the rubrics that you are co-constructing with them (see Practice 12).

HOW WE CONSOLIDATE A LESSON IN A THINKING CLASSROOM

Practice 10

Consolidation of the group activity is the same as in the anchor book. But, for the part where students are all working on different topics and sequences of tasks, consolidation cannot happen at the whole-group level. The curricular work is often too fractured for that to work. Instead, you need to do the consolidation for individuals or groups of students. Obviously, this is not something that can happen at the end of the session. It needs to be a continuous and ongoing part of every interaction you have with the students in the room. When you are giving a group a hint on one, take the opportunity to consolidate some of the ideas from the previous tasks that they have already worked through. Pull students together who are working on similar tasks and go through an impromptu consolidation of what they have learned so far in the session and so on. Do not feel that you have to do it for everyone. Some things are just not possible in these settings.

TOOLKITS

In a setting where independent self-paced learners come together from time to time, all 14 practices are still relevant. Some can be executed as usual; others need adaptations. Also in need of adaptation are the orders with which these practices are implemented and the toolkits into which they cluster (see Figure 8.1).

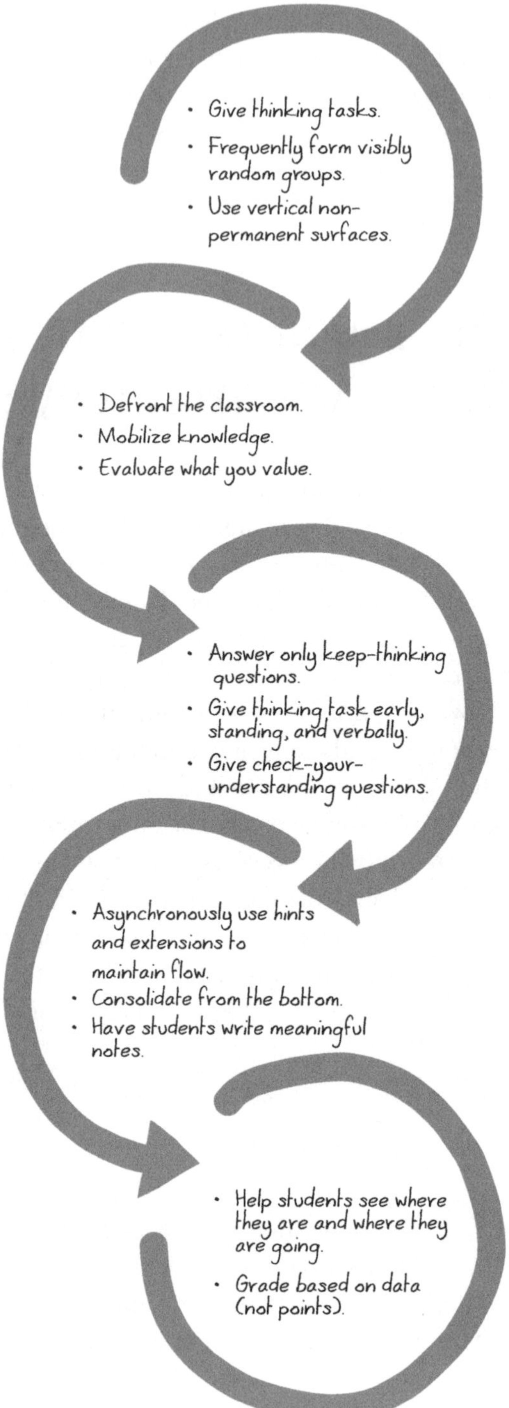

- Give thinking tasks.
- Frequently form visibly random groups.
- Use vertical non-permanent surfaces.

- Defront the classroom.
- Mobilize knowledge.
- Evaluate what you value.

- Answer only keep-thinking questions.
- Give thinking task early, standing, and verbally.
- Give check-your-understanding questions.

- Asynchronously use hints and extensions to maintain flow.
- Consolidate from the bottom.
- Have students write meaningful notes.

- Help students see where they are and where they are going.
- Grade based on data (not points).

Figure 8.1   Toolkits for Building a Thinking Classroom for Independent Learning

9

BUILDING A THINKING CLASSROOM FOR HOMESCHOOLING

. . . .

Homeschooling is something that has become increasingly popular over the last decade and includes a wide range of possible educational structures, some of which have the student learning from home while being enrolled in courses that are delivered from a distance. We have looked at a number of examples of these types of course structures in this supplement—see Chapters 4, 5, and 8. In these settings, a parent, guardian, or private instructor may be supporting the learner as they work their way through the course content. This support is most often described as one-on-one tutoring and, as described in Chapter 12, can be enhanced with the use of some of the thinking classroom practices.

In other forms of homeschooling, the learner is working under the guidance of a parent, guardian, or private instructor who is responsible for both designing and delivering the learning experiences. In some cases, there are specified curricular outcomes to guide this planning, and in other cases, they have the freedom to craft their own curriculum. In this chapter, I discuss how, even in these one-on-one homeschool settings where the learner is not enrolled in an outside course, a thinking classroom can be built. To do so, however, will require the modification of eight of the thinking classroom practices, with the rest being enacted as described in the anchor book. If you have more than one learner at home, some of the ideas from Chapter 11 may be relevant here as well.

HOW GROUPS ARE FORMED IN A THINKING CLASSROOM

Practice 2

If you want to build a thinking classroom within the homeschooling environment, then the most important thing that you need to do is to build a collaborative relationship with the learner. This is not easy to do as it will require you to occupy the role both of teacher and co-learner. One way to make this easier is to establish right from the start that when doing think tasks, you are a learner and a collaborator. And when doing other things like assessment, you are the teacher.

WHAT TYPES OF TASKS WE USE IN A THINKING CLASSROOM

Practice 1

The tasks that you use in this setting are the same as would be used in any thinking classroom (see the anchor book). Begin with non-curricular tasks to build the culture of thinking—and in this setting, the collaborative nature of your relationship. When you think you are both ready for it, move to curricular tasks.

Although you may be creating these tasks yourself, it is important that you don't reveal this. Pretend that they come from an outside source and that you don't always have access to the answers. This will make it easier for you to establish and sustain your role as a collaborator when working on thinking tasks. If your learner sees you as the source of the tasks, then they will continuously try to reposition you as a teacher during these times.

WHEN, WHERE, AND HOW TASKS ARE GIVEN IN A THINKING CLASSROOM

Practice 6

Like in a normal thinking classroom, give the tasks early and verbally while standing at the vertical non-permanent surface (VNPS). However, keep in mind that whether it is true or not, you need to keep up the façade that the tasks originate from outside of you—"Okay, so, I saw this thing on Twitter where you start with 12 envelopes . . ." Of course, this is just the tax collector task from Chapter 6 of the anchor book. When you get into the curricular tasks, you can say, "So, here is the list of questions I got from a homeschooling website."

HOW WE ARRANGE THE FURNITURE IN A THINKING CLASSROOM

Practice 4

With there only being one learner, with you operating as a collaborator, and with there not being a classroom, defronting the classroom loses all meaning. But defronting the classroom is only a means to an end. And the end is to introduce enough chaos into the classroom that students perceived it as a safe place to think—to get messy and make mistakes. Defronting the classroom is only one way to achieve this. There are other ways to introduce small amounts of chaos. For example, resist the urge to bring too much order to the VNPS. Allow your learner to wander on the surface and, when you are holding the marker, be deliberate about not being too orderly. Thinking is messy, and the products of thinking are messy. Don't just let that be okay—encourage it.

HOW WE ANSWER QUESTIONS IN A THINKING CLASSROOM

Practice 5

Because you will operate in this environment both as a learner and as a teacher, it will be easy for you to accidentally slip between these roles and start acting like a teacher when you should be acting like a co-learner. Likewise, it will be easy for your learner to reposition your role within this setting. The most common example of this is when, during a thinking activity that you are collaborating on, they turn to you and ask you a question as if you are the teacher. This can be a stop-thinking question or a keep-thinking question. Regardless of what type of question it is, it is very important that you respond to it as a groupmate and not as the teacher. So, if they ask, "Is this right?" respond with, "I don't know. Is there a way we can check if it is?" Or, if they ask, "What do we do next?" say, "I'm not sure. Why don't we check the sheet to see what the next question is?" Notice the use of the word *we*. This repositions the authority in your response from *you* as a teacher to *we* as partners.

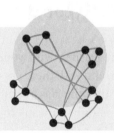

HOW WE FOSTER STUDENT AUTONOMY IN A THINKING CLASSROOM

Practice 8

One of the consequences of this role-play as a collaborator is that there is now no source of knowledge in the room to refer to if the "group" gets stuck. There is no other groups' work to look at and there is no "teacher" to ask. To compensate for this, you will need to build up a repertoire of other resources that can be accessed in the moment. This could be anything from Photomath to Wolfram Alpha® and a host of other apps and websites where answers can be gotten. Like in any thinking classroom, however, having access to resources is not the same thing as accessing these resources. You will have to work with your learner to build up the autonomy to reach out to these sources if and when necessary. As a co-learner, it will be easy for you to suggest that "we check our answer on Photomath."

HOW WE CONSOLIDATE A LESSON IN A THINKING CLASSROOM

Practice 10

Working from the position of co-learner, it will not be possible for you to lead consolidation. But you can still request one for yourself, "Okay. Explain that to me one more time. How is this one different from the others we did?" You can also position the consolidation as a reflection: "So, what did we learn today?" Regardless of how you prompt it, once the consolidation begins you can add to it, "Right. And then we did the case where the answer was greater than one and we had to regroup." You can also make corrections as needed: "Wait. I thought we decided that it is more efficient to add the whole number part first and then the fraction part."

This reflection can also be guided toward processes rather than content. For example, you can draw attention to strategies: "So, that was a good strategy we used there. I think we should try to remember that for next time. What should we call it?" Or you can draw attention to the collective autonomy: "Which method for checking our answer did you like the best?"

WHAT WE CHOOSE TO EVALUATE IN A THINKING CLASSROOM

Practice 12

Evaluating what you value is still relevant in the homeschooling context. But, because you will play the role of collaborator while working on the task, you can then not evaluate the behaviors discussed in Chapter 12 of the anchor book. Having said that, you can co-construct rubrics together for things like how well your learner is doing check-your-understanding questions or making meaningful notes—two practices in which you play the role of teacher.

To build a thinking classroom in a homeschooling environment requires you to bifurcate your roles. You need to be the teacher when enacting things like check-your-understanding questions, meaningful notes, and all forms of assessment. But you should play the role of co-learner for the practices that support the collaborative work on thinking tasks. This will require you to make shifts in the ways you enact these practices as well as the order you implement them (see Figure 9.1).

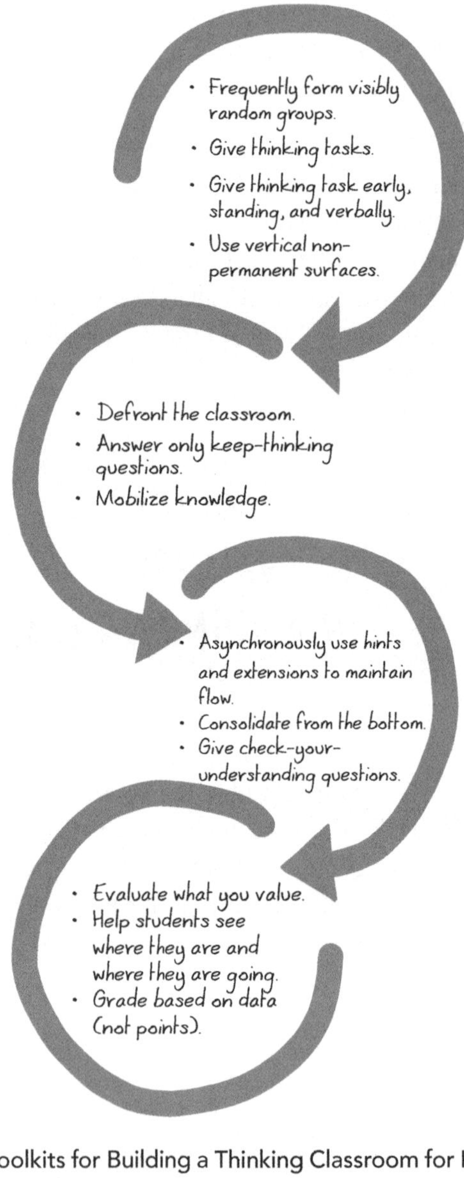

- Frequently form visibly random groups.
- Give thinking tasks.
- Give thinking task early, standing, and verbally.
- Use vertical non-permanent surfaces.

- Defront the classroom.
- Answer only keep-thinking questions.
- Mobilize knowledge.

- Asynchronously use hints and extensions to maintain flow.
- Consolidate from the bottom.
- Give check-your-understanding questions.

- Evaluate what you value.
- Help students see where they are and where they are going.
- Grade based on data (not points).

Figure 9.1 Toolkits for Building a Thinking Classroom for Homeschooling

CATEGORY 5

SUPPORTING LEARNERS

10

SUPPORTING STUDENTS WITH UNFINISHED LEARNING OF PREVIOUS CONCEPTS IN A THINKING CLASSROOM

- -

Ever present in our classrooms, whether thinking classrooms or not, is a persistent and pervasive need to help individual students with their unfinished learning. Whether they come to you at the beginning of the school year with gaps in their learning or they fail to fully reify learning within your classroom, these students are going to need your help to fill in their gaps or to pull together their ideas. In this chapter, I look at how to provide this help when students have unfinished learning from concepts covered previously, whether from the current school year or previous school years.

Our research shows that enacting a thinking classroom helps with this in a variety of ways. First, the collaborative nature of thinking classrooms fills the room with resources that help compensate for any one student's unfinished learning, giving them the ability to move forward with new learning while also affording them the extra time needed for unfinished learning to get backfilled. This backfilling is supported by the ubiquitous peer-to-peer discussions that permeate the thinking classroom. In short, thinking classrooms give students time, resources, redundancy, and peers to help them finish their learning.

But this will not solve all problems all the time, and you, as the teacher, will probably still need to step in and facilitate a process that will help students finish their learning. And, as is often the case with unfinished learning, different students have different gaps and will require individualized support from you. The thinking classroom has six practices that can help you provide individualized support for small numbers of students at a time, and I present them here in the order that they would occur in the intervention. But they will need some modification in order to become an effective aid to you within this setting. To be clear, this is a context that is embedded within a thinking classroom structure as described in the anchor book. So, what follows is not about how to modify practices for the whole class but rather how to modify them for the specific purpose of helping a number of specific students backfill some of their unfinished learning.

HOW GROUPS ARE FORMED IN A THINKING CLASSROOM

Practice 2

An important distinction for this setting is that this isn't really a collaborative group. It is a collection of individual students with individualized needs working with you at the same time. The first thing that you will need to do is collect some of these students together to work in a common space while the rest of the class is making meaningful notes and working on check-your-understanding questions. Although this could be a single student, for the psychological well-being of the student, it is best if it is more than one. Because each of these students will need individualized help, I suggest you start with two students. When you become comfortable (and proficient) with facilitating two students' unfinished learning at the same time, you can add a third, and then a fourth. I have not seen it work well with more than four students.

WHERE STUDENTS WORK IN A THINKING CLASSROOM

Practice 3

Once you have these students together, you need to give them somewhere to work. Ideally, it would be good to have them working on separate vertical non-permanent surfaces (VNPSs). This would give you an easy view of how each student is progressing. However, the students might feel self-conscious about working on their unfinished learning on a surface that the rest of their classmates can see. The best alternative to this is to have them work on horizontal non-permanent surfaces (HNPS) like a personal whiteboard or suitable proxy. Having the students sit with you around a table while they work on these personal HNPSs will still allow you to monitor their progress while not drawing attention to their work on unfinished learning.

WHEN, WHERE, AND HOW TASKS ARE GIVEN IN A THINKING CLASSROOM

Practice 6

Even though the students are working individually, you should still strive to give the tasks verbally and to get them thinking on a task quickly. This means that if there is something that you wish to explain to one of the students, you need to condense it down to its bare essence so they can get started quickly. This is even truer if there are different instructions that you need to give to different students. If you have more to share, save it for hints and extensions (Practice 9) and consolidation (Practice 10).

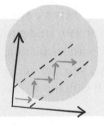

HOW WE USE HINTS AND EXTENSIONS IN A THINKING CLASSROOM

Practice 9

Once you have gathered these students together, you need to take each of them through an individualized and thin-sliced flow-sequence of tasks on the concepts that they are struggling with. For example, you may have one student working on a sequence of tasks on adding fractions and another student working on a sequence of multiplying decimal tasks. Regardless of the concept, you start by giving each student the first task from their personal sequence and then provide individualized hints and extensions to them as they move through the tasks. If their ability has increased to the point where they can handle the next challenge, you increase the difficulty. If it has not, you give them a parallel task to the one they just completed. This will allow you to more clearly tailor the hints and extensions needed to maximize their engagement, thinking, and learning.

HOW WE ANSWER QUESTIONS IN A THINKING CLASSROOM

Practice 5

This is a setting where you are trying to be highly supportive and nurturing of the learning that is going on. You are individualizing the tasks, hints, and extensions as well as the consolidations, and the assumption will be that you will also answer all questions. But this is not the case. Remember that thinking is a necessary precursor to learning, and as supportive as we are being, the goal is still to keep them thinking. Answer all their keep-thinking questions. But if they ask a stop-thinking question, push back on it in such a way that you not only put them back into the role of thinking:

- What do you think?

- What are some other possibilities?

- Why do you think that didn't work?

but also keep the language inclusive to maintain their productive struggle:

- Is there a way for us to check that?

- Let's try that and see what happens.

- Okay. Where do you think we went wrong?

Having said that, you have to carefully monitor their frustration level. If you see this beginning to climb, diffuse it with an answer that reduces the challenge of the task at hand and brings them back into the flow.

HOW WE CONSOLIDATE A LESSON IN A THINKING CLASSROOM

Practice 10

Unlike in the larger thinking classroom structure where consolidation comes at the end of the sequence, in this setting you consolidate continuously with each student. Depending on at what pace they are moving through the tasks, and when they finish a task in relation to other students, this may mean that you are consolidating after each task or after a few tasks. While you are consolidating a task (or tasks) with one student, you will also be giving the extensions to others as they finish. This will require some patience on the other students' part, but it has been shown to work well in this very focused and calm setting.

TOOLKIT

This setting within a setting is an important and effective way to help students with unfinished learning. It is different from a more general thinking classroom setting in that the students' available and accessible resources have been reduced to just you. On the flip side, the resources you are providing in this space are ideally positioned to provide the scaffolding and support that the student requires without, at the same time, diminishing their need to think. The six aforementioned practices and their modification will need to all be enacted at once and will help you provide this support while helping you maintain the rigor of a thinking classroom (see Figure 10.1).

- Frequently form visibly random groups.
- Use vertical non-permanent surfaces.
- Give thinking task early, standing, and verbally.
- Asynchronously use hints and extensions to maintain flow.
- Answer only keep-thinking questions.
- Consolidate from the bottom.

Figure 10.1 Toolkit for Supporting Learners With Unfinished Learning of Previous Concepts in a Thinking Classroom

11

SUPPORTING STUDENTS WITH UNFINISHED LEARNING OF CURRENT CONCEPTS IN A THINKING CLASSROOM

• •

Sometimes in a thinking classroom, one member of a group may begin to fall behind their groupmates. Our research shows that in a well-functioning thinking classroom, if this happens the group will rebalance itself by encouraging and responding to questions, moving the marker around, and ensuring that everyone has an understanding of the concepts at hand before moving on to the next task. This, coupled with the plethora of inter-group and intra-group resources available in the room, works to minimize the number of students who fall behind the other members of their group. Even in a well-functioning thinking classroom, however, a student may still fall behind, and you may have to intervene. The anchor book offers strategies for dealing with this from moving the marker to the student falling behind to making a rule that the person with the marker cannot write any of their own ideas. You can also intervene and do a mini-consolidation for the group in order to try to reify some of the learning that is on offer from the task at hand. Usually, and for most students, these efforts by the group and by you work. But sometimes it doesn't. And the student continues to fall behind and does not quite reify all the learning that is available during the group activity. In other situations, the groups are working well, but one group does not get as far into the flow sequence of thin-sliced tasks as you would have liked.

Either way, there is unfinished learning for some of the students in your classroom. In this chapter, I present ways in which you can help these students finish the learning from the current lesson. To be clear, what I am talking about here is different from what was discussed in Chapter 10, which was about unfinished learning from concepts met previously.

Because these gaps cut across a wide range of concepts from the current school year and from years prior, the intervention discussed in Chapter 10 needs to be personalized to each student. The unfinished learning that I discuss here pertains to the concepts covered in your current lesson. As such, the range of unfinished learning among your students is much narrower and offers you the possibility to intervene with these students as a group. Seven practices are relevant to this intervention, and I present them here in the order that they would occur in the intervention. As in Chapter 10, this is a context that is embedded within a thinking classroom structure as described in the anchor book. What follows is not about how to modify practices for the whole class but rather how to modify them for the specific purpose of helping a group of students backfill some of their unfinished learning from the day's activities.

HOW GROUPS ARE FORMED IN A THINKING CLASSROOM

Practice 2

The intervention begins by collecting some of these students to work together in a common space while the rest of the class is making meaningful notes and working on check-your-understanding questions. To leverage the effectiveness of groups, this needs to be a minimum of two students but could be as many as six. Because the range of concepts that you will be supporting these students on is rather narrow, you will form groups of two or, preferably three, students. If there will be more than one group, do this randomly.

WHERE STUDENTS WORK IN A THINKING CLASSROOM

Practice 3

Ideally, you want these groups working on a vertical non-permanent surface (VNPS). But they may feel self-conscious doing so while others are sitting, so you may have to settle for having them work on a horizontal non-permanent surface (HNPS) like a whiteboard, or a suitable proxy, lying flat on a table. If it to be an HNPS, ensure that the students are all sitting in an orientation that will allow them to all see the HNPS from the same orientation—that is, no one is looking at it upside down.

WHEN, WHERE, AND HOW TASKS ARE GIVEN IN A THINKING CLASSROOM

Practice 6

As much as possible, tasks should be given verbally in the first five minutes of the session with the group(s) standing or sitting around the VNPS or HNPS. If you have something that you wish to explain to the learner before they begin the first task, condense it down to its bare essence so the groups can get started. If you have more to share, save it for hints and extensions (Practice 9) and consolidation (Practice 10).

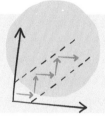

HOW WE USE HINTS AND EXTENSIONS IN A THINKING CLASSROOM

Practice 9

In essence, you will have this group of students work on a flow-sequenced set of tasks built around the concept(s) pertaining to their unfinished learning from the day. The difference is that the sequence has to begin with a task that is simple enough that they can all approach it. For example, if they are struggling with adding fractions with different denominators, start the sequence with common denominators:

$$\frac{3}{7} + \frac{2}{7} = \qquad \frac{4}{9} + \frac{3}{9} = \qquad \frac{4}{5} + \frac{3}{5} =$$

The first two tasks are familiar ground and will help build confidence and get the group(s) working together. The third task will require a bit more thinking while still staying with concepts that they know—common denominators. From here you can shift to tasks such as

$$\frac{1}{2} + \frac{1}{4} = \qquad \frac{1}{4} + \frac{3}{8} = \qquad \frac{1}{2} + \frac{5}{8} =$$

The fourth task is likely familiar to the students just from ongoing exposure to halves and quarters in previous grades or real life and provides a space where they can begin to formalize some of their tacit thinking. The fifth question pushes them and will require them to begin to establish a common denominator while, at the same time, not making it too difficult to do so. The sixth task repeats this requirement while also requiring them to think about what they did in task 3. From here you can move to tasks where the denominators are relatively prime and then to where they are not relatively prime but one denominator is not a multiple of the other. In essence, you are taking the group(s) through a thin-sliced flow sequence of tasks that starts easier and moves slower than the sequence you used for the whole-class part of the lesson.

Your job during all this goes well beyond providing the sequence of tasks, however. While they are working, you are going to be there the whole time, providing hints and extensions as needed to keep the group(s) in flow. This may mean that you move them up to the next level of challenge as they finish or, if their ability has not yet fully developed at the level they are at, giving them a parallel task to the one they just finished.

Practice 5

HOW WE ANSWER QUESTIONS IN A THINKING CLASSROOM

As in Chapter 4, this is a structure wherein you are maximizing your support and optimizing the scaffolding. The sequence of tasks starts simply and moves as slow as it needs to. You are providing continuous hints and extensions as well as ongoing consolidation. So, the assumption will be that you will also answer all their questions. But this is not the case. Thinking is a necessary precursor to learning and, as such, you have to keep them thinking. So, answer their keep-thinking questions, but deflect their stop-thinking questions:

- What do you think?

- What are some other possibilities?

- Why do you think that didn't work?

but also keep the language inclusive to maintain their productive struggle:

- Is there a way for us to check that?

- Let's try that and see what happens.

- Okay. Where do you think we went wrong?

Having said that, you have to carefully monitor their frustration level. If you see this beginning to climb, diffuse it with an answer that reduces the challenge of the task at hand and brings them back into the flow.

HOW WE CONSOLIDATE A LESSON IN A THINKING CLASSROOM

Practice 10

Unlike in the larger thinking classroom structure, where consolidation comes at the end of the sequence of tasks, in this specific setting you consolidate with the group after each task. As soon as they finish a task, step in and reify what they did by noticing and naming the key steps they did to complete the task. For example, after they finish the first task, you may say something like "Okay. So you noticed that the denominators were the same *[circle the denominators]*, so all you needed to do was add the numerators *[circle the sum of the numerators]*. Good. Okay, here is the next one." You would then give them the next task and move the marker to a different student.

This ongoing consolidation allows you to draw attention to what the students are doing well—which helps them see that they are capable while at the same time adding formal language and structures and highlighting what aspects are important—the need for a common denominator.

WHAT HOMEWORK LOOKS LIKE IN A THINKING CLASSROOM

Practice 7

Once you have moved through the flow-sequenced tasks that you have planned for this group, keep them together in the same location, but give them a set of check-your-understanding tasks for them to complete individually. This set of tasks should be sequenced in the same way as the tasks they just completed as a group. The goal here is to immediately transfer the collective knowing and doing to individual knowing and doing. In many ways, this will shift the environment to the one that was described in Chapter 4. The difference is, however, that the students should be more independent as they are operating on the immediacy of their collective success.

TOOLKIT

When students have unfinished learning from the day's lesson, the variance in their individual needs is small enough that you can work with them simultaneously and collectively. This work can be supported by modifying and enacting seven of the thinking classroom practices. The nature of this work requires that all seven of these practices are enacted together (see Figure 11.1).

- Frequently form visibly random groups.
- Use vertical non-permanent surfaces.
- Give thinking task early, standing, and verbally.
- Asynchronously use hints and extensions to maintain flow.
- Answer only keep-thinking questions.
- Consolidate from the bottom.
- Give check-your-understanding questions.

Figure 11.1 Toolkit for Supporting Learners With Unfinished Learning of Current Concepts in a Thinking Classroom

12

SUPPORTING STUDENTS THROUGH ONE-ON-ONE TEACHING USING THINKING CLASSROOM PRACTICES

. . . .

Whether you are a teacher working one-on-one with a student, a parent working at home with your child, or a tutor working with a client and whether you are working on backfilling unfinished learning or providing an enrichment activity, thinking is still a necessary precursor to learning. If your learner is not thinking, they are not learning. This chapter is about the thinking classroom practices you can bring into this environment and how you need to modify them for the specific context of working one-on-one with a learner. There are six practices that are relevant, and I present them here in the order that they would play out within this unique setting of working one-on-one with a learner.

WHERE STUDENTS WORK IN A THINKING CLASSROOM

Practice 3

Even though the learner is working alone, the best workspace is still a vertical non-permanent surface (VNPS). The non-permanent nature of the workspace will encourage the learner to risk sooner and risk longer. And having them stand while working ensures more active engagement. The only possible exception to this is if the learner is in a classroom full of other students. If you are working with this learner on new learning or enrichment, then the VNPS is still a possibility.

If, however, you are working with a student in need of one-on-one support with unfinished learning then a horizontal non-permanent surface (HNPS) would be more appropriate as this does not draw as much attention to the fact that the learner is in need of extra help.

WHEN, WHERE, AND HOW TASKS ARE GIVEN IN A THINKING CLASSROOM

Practice 6

As in a normal thinking classroom, as much as possible, tasks are given verbally and in the first five minutes of the session. So, if you have something that you wish to explain to the learner before they begin the first task, you need to condense this down to its bare essence so they can get started. Remember that the goal is to offer only what is needed for them to start the first task. If you feel that there is more to share, save this for hints and extensions (Practice 9) and consolidation (Practice 10).

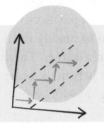

HOW WE USE HINTS AND EXTENSIONS IN A THINKING CLASSROOM

Practice 9

When working one-on-one with an individual learner, regardless of the context, your main job is to take them through a thin-sliced flow sequence of tasks on the concept(s) you are supporting them on. If this is an enrichment activity, then the first task can still be quite challenging and the slices can be thicker. For example, if a student is seeking some extended learning around the unusual baker sequence of tasks presented in Chapter 9 of the anchor book, you might wish to start an enrichment activity by asking the student to redo all the questions but with a twist. Rather than calculate what fraction of the whole cake each piece is, ask them how much should be charged for each piece if the goal is to earn $20 from each cake. Once they have completed this, you can ask them how much each piece would cost for the cake in Figure 12.1 and so on.

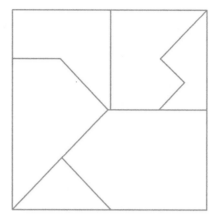

Figure 12.1 An Unusually Cut Cake

If the learner is working on unfinished learning, as in Chapters 10 and 11, the first task in the sequence should be simple and the slices should be thin. For example, if the student was having difficulty turning a linear relationship into an algebraic expression, then the sequence might look something like this:

1. 1, 2, 3, 4, 5, . . .

2. 2, 3, 4, 5, 6, . . .

3. 0, 1, 2, 3, 4, . . .

4. 2, 4, 6, 8, 10, . . .

5. 5, 10, 15, 20, 25, . . .

6. 4, 7, 10, 13, 16, . . .

7. 8, 10, 12, 14, 16, . . .

8. . . .

The first one of these is very simple ($y = x$) and puts a direct relationship between the position of the term and the value of the term. The second task offsets this relationship by +1, resulting in $y = x + 1$. The third offsets the relationship the other way (−1), giving $y = x - 1$. The differences between these tasks are incremental, designed to help the learner feel successful at every step.

While the learner moves through this sequence, your job will be to provide hints and extensions as needed to maintain flow. This may mean that you move them up to the next level of challenge as they finish or, if their ability has not yet fully developed at the level they are at, giving them a parallel task to the one they just finished.

HOW WE ANSWER QUESTIONS IN A THINKING CLASSROOM

Practice 5

In this one-on-one setting, you are controlling every aspect of the learner's experience. You are providing the sequence of tasks, hints, and extensions. And you are doing so in an effort to build a positive learning experience. This, however, does not mean that you answer all their questions. It is important to remember that in this setting, like all other settings, thinking is a necessary precursor to learning. So, if they ask a stop-thinking question, push back on it in such a way that you put them back into the role of thinking:

- What do you think?
- Is there a way for us to check that?
- Let's try that and see what happens.
- What are some other possibilities?
- Okay. Where do you think we went wrong?
- Why do you think that didn't work?

In the case of unfinished learning, you still need to monitor their frustration level. If you see this beginning to climb, diffuse it with an answer that reduces the challenge of the task at hand and brings them back into the flow. For enrichment settings, you still need to monitor the learner for signs of frustration, but keep in mind that you do not want to rob them of the opportunity to persevere.

HOW WE CONSOLIDATE A LESSON IN A THINKING CLASSROOM

Practice 10

For cases of unfinished learning, your job will also be to provide ongoing and continuous consolidation after each task by reifying what they did by noticing and naming the key aspects of each task. For example, after they finish the first task, you may step in and say something like "Okay. So you noticed that the positions of each term x are equal to the value of each term y. Good. Okay, here is the next one."

You would then give them the next task. This ongoing consolidation allows you to draw attention to what the learner is doing well—which helps them see that they are capable while at the same time adding formal language and structures and highlighting what aspects are important—the need to relate and position to value. If you are working with a learner on enrichment tasks, the consolidation can happen less frequently and can, in fact, involve the learner telling you what the salient and important aspects of the tasks are.

HOW WE USE FORMATIVE ASSESSMENT IN A THINKING CLASSROOM

Practice 13

In the case of unfinished learning, once you have moved through the flow-sequenced tasks that you have planned for the learner, give them a set of tasks for them to complete on their own. When they are done, go over these with them and have them self-assess and record their performance on a navigation instrument to document where they are (what they are able to do correctly on their own) and where they are going (what they are not yet able to do correctly on their own). Use this to celebrate progress as well as plan for further one-on-one learning.

TOOLKIT

The one-on-one learning environment can be an effective way to either support learning with concepts they are challenged by or to provide enrichment opportunities for an individual learner. Since the goal is for them to learn, then you are going to have to get them to think and then support them in this thinking. The toolkit for this setting comprises six tools and they are all enacted at once (see Figure 12.2).

- Use vertical non-permanent surfaces.
- Give thinking task early, standing, and verbally.
- Asynchronously use hints and extensions to maintain flow.
- Answer only keep-thinking questions.
- Consolidate from the bottom.
- Help students see where they are and where they are going.

Figure 12.2   Toolkit for Supporting Students Through One-on-One Teaching Using Thinking Classroom Practices

INDEX

Keep learning...
with Peter Liljedahl

KEEP THINKING ... KEEP LEARNING

Much of what happens in math classrooms today is guided by institutional norms laid down at the inception of an industrial-age model of public education. These norms have enabled a culture of teaching and learning that is often devoid of student thinking. This book presents the results of more than 15 years of research on which teaching practices are effective for getting students to think and which ones are not. *Building Thinking Classrooms in Mathematics* takes you through a step-by-step approach that you can use to transform your classroom from a space where students mimic to a space where students think.

Now Available: Supplement to modify the 14 practices for different settings.

Walk the talk of a thinking classroom.

Peter Liljedahl offers a range of highly engaging and interactive workshop experiences on a variety of building thinking classroom topics, including Introduction to the Thinking Classroom, Assessment for a Thinking Classroom, Building Thinking Classrooms in Different Settings, Increasing Student Responsibility in a Thinking Classroom, and Equity and Diversity in a Thinking Classroom. Each of these topics can be pursued through a single workshop or series of workshops, in person or virtually.

Visit **buildingthinkingclassrooms.com/consulting/** for further information and contacts.

CORWIN **Mathematics**

CMN21748

A SAGE Publishing Company

Helping educators make the greatest impact

CORWIN HAS ONE MISSION: to enhance education through intentional professional learning.

We build long-term relationships with our authors, educators, clients, and associations who partner with us to develop and continuously improve the best evidence-based practices that establish and support lifelong learning.